"What Ho!"

love

freddie! x

'What Ho! Giotto'

Freddie Owen

An artist's verbal sketchbook,
on life, love of Italy
and the creation of a garden and studio
in Le Marche

Paintings and drawings by the author
© Copyright 2013 Freddie Owen all rights reserved
ISBN 978 – 1 – 300 – 87135 – 4

FOR LAURIE AND MERI
WHO ENHANCED
THE JOURNEY

'What Ho! Giotto'

i) SEEDS AND NEEDS

ii) ROOTS AND SHOOTS

iii) SNOWING AND GROWING

iv) PESTS AND GUESTS

v) RETCHING AND SKETCHING

vi) FUN AND SUN

SEEDS AND NEEDS

It is high summer here in Le Marche, Italy. As I look out through a flaccid fly-blind and flailing oleander to the church tower of San Giovanni dripping with rain, I feel the strange urge to write. I normally express myself in paint but at the moment, to revive an old Renaissance quip; it's 'too *bagnato* (wet) even for *l'acquarello* (water-colours)'! We're halfway through August and it has been raining for over a fortnight – it's a long way from my deeply engrained vision of Italy.

We have experienced so many hot Italian summers as a family. Like the one in Arezzo where, after our humours had been warmed by the hatted people of Piero della Francesca's frescoes, we came out into such a furnace of a day that if it hadn't been for Vasari's shaded portico we would still be spot-welded to the pavement. That feeling of desperate thirst in an Italian town just after lunch when everything is closed, can give one just a small inkling of what it must be like to be stuck in the gob-less Gobi desert.

There have been more occasions of near expiration due to the intense heat in Italy, than anywhere else, times when the countryside has gone beyond dry and it looks as if the vegetation could be bagged up for 'crispy nibbles'... when the cooked land is so monotone, that seen in moonlight it looks no different from daylight. We've seen landscapes in a Tuscan summer that could have been ' white on white' canvases or vistas with no horizon, where the tone of the land and sky was so similar it was as though the boundary-line had been stolen by the heat.

When the sun has parched your gullet to cracked stucco with rays that crazy-pave your skin like *tesserae* and your vocal chords need to be plunged into a builder's hod of ice to pitch a note, you know what an Italian summer is - or so I thought until now...

We have had this artist's retreat for five years and this is the first time that my consciousness has bubbled to the surface to ask the question ' why am I here? ' - I mean particularly here - in Italy. Perhaps the drumming of the incessant rain has induced some kind of trance-like state, or maybe it is the first time there's been a moment to think about it, we certainly seemed to have been drawn here, beyond our will. What I had dreamed of from childhood (an impossible fantasy, far beyond reach) was to have a little pergola in the sun, maybe even grow an olive tree - and certainly not to have another moist corner in my life. I'm not really even ' for ' the ownership of property that is surplus to requirements, and am still unsure if the realisation of a dream is a good thing either. So where did the motivation come from to drive us, in our middle ages, towards this damp DIY Nirvana?

For me the very word 'Italy' has been a sensory knob that can be twiddled at will, for pleasure. I don't even have to be here - it induces the same clichéd, Pavlovian thrill as that first *Cornetto*, a climaxing aria from il Trovatore or the taste of a *Lacrima* wine - that feels so like dragging your tongue over a shaggy herb bed.

Of course, there are also the usual corny culprits of Italianate mind-moulding that have lured so many before me. One of many possible sample lists:

Canaletto... Rossini... Puccini... Fellini... Fettuccini. 'Death in Venice'... 'A Room with a View' and 'Vroom with a View' that scene in 'The English Patient' where the girl is swung in front of the fresco... ' Enchanted April'... Kenneth Branagh's wedding scene in 'Much Ado'... 'A Tuscan Childhood'... 'Stealing Beauty'... 'After Hannibal'... 'Under the Tuscan Sun'... maybe even 'A Place in the Sun'... 'Tea with Mussolini' (or for some people, I suppose, even Mussolini himself).

These representations of an ideal Italy have certainly filled a small pool in my brain-hole, into which it's possible to dip a toe, willy-nilly. I had been persuaded into thinking that Italy is a place to be lived in soft focus - but, of course, with perfectly *al dente* pasta - a place, where the Eternal Flame was fuelled by extra virgin olive oil and where ample food and drink didn't lead to obesity (just look at the beauty of the young).

I realise now that I had succumbed to over-romantic visions of Italy very early in life, without even being aware of it; when only three years old, my Great-Aunt Rene showed me how to paint the stripy poles that line the canals of Venice, (she had been on some of those first charabanc tours of Europe in the Twenties and Thirties). I still paint them occasionally today, and every time I do so, it takes me back to her trying to keep me occupied when I was ill, spoiling me with ' milk-sops ' (bread soaked in milk) and Lucozade - the infant equivalent of pasta and prosecco maybe?

My first real brushes with the country were indeed idyllic. Italy obviously has a tremendous amount to offer a painter; the artistic heritage of the Etruscans and Romans; the *Trecento* through to the *Seicento* - the magnificent Renaissance in art and architecture. But the cultural history is not the only inspiration - there is of course the landscape itself.

Much of the scenery is still the same as it was in the backgrounds of the early religious paintings, and can be seen on any drive through Le Marche, Umbria or Tuscany - those gradated blue skies a backdrop to oddly-shaped mountains, dotted with umbrella pines and cypresses, and still peopled with the genetically familiar faces from the frescoes of Cimabue, Giotto, Benozzo Gozzoli and the rest - the characters from the paintings can be seen alive and well (as if they've just been granted five minutes off by the artist) at any of today's many historical pageants such as the flag throwing in Fabriano, the *Palio* in Siena or the *Quintana* in Ascoli Piceno. Italians who love dressing up, pose on street corners, smoking fags tilted on one hip and wearing chequer-board patterned or two-toned tights, like figures from a Signorelli fresco but with a mobile phone where a codpiece should sit. Or they can be seen riding their scooters through narrow alleyways at breakneck speeds, their medieval headgear wrapping around an infant, or even an ancient *nonna* riding pillion. It doesn't take long to get used to seeing strange juxtapositions of fashion history: tabards with tattoos, ruffs with Ray-Bans.... or bodice laces with pierced faces.

My wife, Fiona, and I realised quite early in our children's lives (Laurie son, and Meri daughter) that being freed from the constraints of regular employment gave us one huge advantage; each year we had an open void - the summer, which we were free to fill with adventure. We were always willing to make the most of our trips in a romantic sense, turning the most mundane journey into an odyssey: A voyage to Ireland on a ferry could take on an epic Brendan-esque quality. Sometimes we would get carried away with the anticipation. On our first trip in our Citroën 2CV up to Scotland, we had to start out in the middle of the night, because we were too excited to sleep. By the time we had reached Birmingham (only fifty miles), we'd eaten all the sandwiches that had been prepared for the entire day's drive.

We ventured across Europe a few years later, and by then the romantic expectation of the expeditions was on a par with Paddy Leigh Fermor, the Newbys or even Phileas Fogg, and we pushed just a bit further with each foray. We then realised that it was possible to take a house somewhere foreign for a month or two, funds perm-itting. And, of course, seeing new places is an important part of our work as painters - finding new source material for work justified our travel and time away from home.

Every summer we explored a different part of Europe or beyond. It was an education for all of us - it broadened our minds, and the different delicious foods and wines certainly broadened my waistline.

We had adventures in France, taking six weeks to drive across the South. We stayed beside an azure lake in Bauduen for a month, then a haunted house in the Gorge du Tarn and on to the vineyards of Bergerac. Another tour took us to a friend's twin-towered *pigeonniere* near Cahor, always sketching daily.

But however magnificent and sunny France, Spain, Portugal, Greece, Morocco and Turkey are, we were seeking something extra. I suppose we wanted the Mediterranean 'with knobs on'. Not just the sun and all that comes with it, but more of a cultural *chiaroscuro*. That heady mix of truffle and turpentine, paint and *porcini*, that only one place could offer us. It's strange when I think back, because it took us years to actually go to the one place that we knew, subconsciously, was waiting for us - it was as if we were saving the best bit till last. Then, having finally broken some invisible barrier, we just kept returning to our Spiritual Home - summer after summer we were drawn to the source of the light we needed, to that tiny glow at the end of the tunnel under Monte Bianco - to Italy.

We all kept visual journals, much like a writer might keep written notes of trips. Daily drawings - scenes of vineyards, olive groves, rows of cypresses, and sunlight. Sketching somewhere is the best way to truly understand the detail and spirit of a place, and also have physical involvement with one's environment. It is possible to become familiar with a foreign land, at a deeper level if you've explored its contours and culture with a pencil. After all, the view in front of you, every leaf, shadow and sheen has gone through a kind of mental filter before it hits the paper. What appears on the page is the distillation of the senses. It's a boot-leg recording of one's surroundings - intense, potent and moment capturing. Photographs are a useful way of snapping an instant too, but they just don't give you the whole picture.

Light, landscape and local wines were embibed with an

unquenchable thirst. Visiting as many *pinacoteche* (art galleries) as we could, it was easy to immerse ourselves for weeks at a time in the world of the altar-piece maker or fresco painter. The thrill of discovering a well-loved painting from a book, 'in the flesh', is something we all shared. We were a family in shock the first time we saw Botticelli's *La Primavera* at the Uffizi in Florence, it was so much more powerful and impressive, close up, than any reproduction could ever be.

A friend once asked if our children ever became bored, trailing around cultural sites, but I don't think they did, perhaps because it was the only life they knew, and also because their days were interspersed with a variety of other experiences too. We didn't make a big deal out of visiting galleries, or seeing a special wall painting in a church - the original painters of these incredible works of art probably wouldn't have wanted them to be viewed in hushed reverence, or they wouldn't have added humorous and human bits in the corners, like whimsical fish, men in odd nappy-like underwear, or dogs licking their bollocks.

On one of our six or seven week trips, we were very fortunate to stay next to a converted, presbytery belonging to a couple of English émigrés who had given up the "good life" in swinging London to lead a more challenging life of self-sufficiency in the Italian countryside, near Cagli.

Richard and Peter had moved out of London in their mid thirties and combined resources to buy a place in Italy. Their aim was to live more or less off the land, supplementing their income by doing up their property for holiday rentals. They wanted to live a back to nature lifestyle, but in a mad Englishmen-with-dogs way. They were a new generation of ex-pat/non-pat, not really fitting into any stereotype.

Richard, once a Barrister, now spatchcocked chickens with alacrity, kept bees, mowed between the vines and ran a productive *orto* to provide vegetables. He sang in the local choir and quickly learned to speak perfect Italian (including those strange 'Shakespearian' tenses). It seemed to me, one of the few things he hadn't succeeded in doing was to make his pig's-lard soap become a household name.

Peter, from being successful in theatrical publicity, now took centre stage amongst the vines and vegetables, performing cantina-filling shows of twisted garlic , rows of onions, bottled passata, hanging hams, home-brewed wine by the gallon and oddly-shaped gourds, just for amusement.

Quite some double act.

We stayed in a cottage in the grounds of the old presbytery with its original chapel still intact, complete with confessional box. We first entered the cottage on a blisteringly hot day in July, walking into the welcome cool of the *cucina*. On the table was a bottle of homegrown *vino bianco*, and a bowl of fresh honeycombs, with amber strings webbing to the rim. Their old mongrels, Bobby and Zappa looked on but didn't cross the threshold. They sat, willing titbits to come their way, tails wagging limply in the heat.

To us, Peter and Richard seemed to have successfully assimilated themselves into a quiet, rural and very conservative community, whilst managing to retain their own cultural identity. Living bilingually at ease, they ate like the locals, mixed with the locals, listened to opera (and also *Abba*, but only when doing the vacuuming). They were able to be both Italian and English quite seamlessly, and balanced both equally. Also, like true ambassadors, they had tried to introduce one of the essentials of British culture into the area - apple crumble (Unfortunately, without success, but then, it has taken 'corn flakes' over thirty years to get a foothold).

In no time at all, they became experts on the region, not only writing the definitive English language guide book of the area, but also designing the official Le Marche website. (This was at a time before most people even knew what a website was), so they were the perfect people to show us the area, and were generous and enthusiastic enough to share their new passion with us. Richard spent a day giving us a guided tour of Le Marche. We went from Jesi (known as 'Milan of Le Marche') to Loreto, (the place where Mary's house; the *Santa Casa di Loreto* is said to have arrived by angel courier from Nazareth, leaving an empty space in *Her* home town, and apparently stopping twice on its way, once in Croatia then in Recanati in Italy. It was a well travelled dwelling by all accounts - and it sounds a little implausible too. However the most peculiar thing is, that scientists have confirmed that the materials used in its construction are actually from the Nazareth area - very strange.)

We took in the many tales of local history, sights, sounds, and tastes of the area, and were ripe for conversion to this seductive way of life. Richard found a little restaurant for lunch. It looked quite dismal from the street but when we walked through it, at the back there was a vine-clad paved area of tables overlooking a spectacular valley. In front of us lay strata like layers of rock terraced vineyards and olive groves, industrious and aesthetic at the same time with blues and rusty hues merging together in the warmth and disappearing into a painterly viridian haze. The blueish green of vines, with the elusive pale under-leaf that together seem to shimmer, set on a background of the earthy red that is their land, are the colours of Italy to me - and maybe that's why they are the colours of its National flag too?

Richard then took us on to the Conero peninsula for ice-creams, we overlooked the scimitar bay at Sirolo, where the sea is a tempera wash of cerulean blue - just the powdery reflection of the perfect sky It was our first trip around Le Marche, and we were seduced by this new discovery.

The first seeds had definitely been cast.

Not that we were idealistic or unrealistic, nor were we seeing too soft focus an image to understand the real picture; having children with you is a good way of making sure you stay well attached to the ground. For one thing, whenever we travelled with our kids, we got to know the local hospitals first, almost before we'd hung up our sun-hats; Meri had such a violent eye infection near Florence, that we were escorted by ambulance, at top speed, to the local *Pronto Soccorso* (Accident & Emergency). Sitting in the waiting room, I soon became aware that people who had come in after us were being seen before us and it was hard not to take it personally. A lady in a white coat came up to me and started speaking very quickly in Italian about a coffee machine or something... *"Signore, macchina, macchina... andiamo!"* she was grabbing me by the sleeve and pulling quite hard. She was really annoying.

"No," I said categorically, and shoved her off, "I'm fine, I *really* do not need a coffee.... *Grazie*."

She humphed loudly, span around and went back into her little office, leaving behind her a strong smell of disinfectant and armpits. Patients continued being seen and I really started to feel as though some kind of injustice was afoot. Streams of people were just coming in and being seen. Was this some kind of personal slight or were they just plain rude, leaving the *estraneo* (stranger) until last?

We waited as Meri's eyes got crustier... I made a mental note of the next people to disappear into the surgery.

" Well, we were definitely here before them, this just isn't right," I thought, but I didn't know what to do about it. I didn't think it would be right to make a scene, after all we were foreigners so we just sat with an aura of injustice surrounding us.

The white-coated lady eventually reappeared, after well over an hour. She was suprised to see us still there, I stood up to plead our case. I didn't have to. This time, she grabbed my arm and man-handled me into the corridor. Shrug as I might she was now taking the upper hand. She pulled me down the corridor and stood me in front of a machine with arrows and *lire* notes printed on it. Rubbing her fingers together under my nose she made the universal gesture of thumbing a bank-note. Then she made me feed the appropriate *lire* note into a machine. It produced a ticket and not the expected cup of coffee. I was very apologetic to the kind, strong and highly scented lady. With the ticket in hand, I sat down again. We were at last, officially in the queue to be seen.

It taught me that ten BBC tapes of *Speak Italian* were not enough. (And it also showed that in Italy, you need a little chit of paper to do almost everything... including, queuing at the deli or buying a quick snack in a service station).

When we finally saw the eye specialist she took one look at Meri's tiny little pink, sore eyes, and said:

"*Ma, lei ha i begli occhi !*" ("but, she has beautiful eyes!")

We hoped the doctor's eyesight was alright, presumably she'd somehow been able to see beyond the puss - anyway she prescribed some drops, and we went away happy. Meri's vampiric look turned slowly back to normal. Her *begli occhi* emerged from their crusty chrysalises like little blue butterflies, as the doctor had predicted.

For me, lessons in patient patience had been learned.

She was not the only one to be ill. Laurie, when he was about twelve, had such a severe throat infection that we had to take him to the local hospital. The antibiotics they prescribed didn't seem to work he was getting worse, running a fever and it was becoming a worry. Richard called a surgeon friend to come out and have a look. The surgeon came especially to the house after his work. He peered down Laurie's inflamed and ulcerated throat using the bedside lamp, then he disappeared downstairs without saying a word. He came back with a glass of grappa. Well, we thought, a bit early for grappa but still, doctor knows best...

"Gargle with this," he said, demonstrating - throwing his head back and making exaggerated gargling noises...

Laurie followed suit, gargled and swallowed and then again...

He opened his mouth and tried to speak- it was the first time he had uttered a sound for a number of days so what came out was primeval and disembodied. Firstly, a kind of " Exorcist" growl, followed by a high-pitched squeak. It was if he was trying to find the right frequency on an old wireless set. Then, from deep inside,

Laurie dragged to the surface an 'Ole man River' drowning groan ...

"There you are," said the handsome surgeon, slapping Laurie on the back... "Cured !" He left the room, never to be seen again, but the grappa had worked - Laurie had taken to that sick bed as a boy and had left it as a man - or at least a boy with a very husky, deep bass voice.

Grappa - something any head-chorister wanting to leave his position should know about. It's 'ball-droppingly' good.

From that moment, Laurie's voice remained bass. A boy with a man's voice - quite strange to behold. Especially for us, who'd lived with his cute treble voice for twelve years. Eventually (in a couple of years), the rest of his physique caught up with his voice. It was fortunate that his voice had been fixed, albeit in a different key, because that night the boys had invited us to the annual choir party in their garden. Richard had joined the choir in the local town several years before and it had proved a good way of getting to know some of the locals.

Long tables had been laid with ironed white cloths, the angular creases stood out like an unfolded map and they were contoured with tree shadows.The tables were already prepared with cutlery and glinting glasses, all polished for the feast. From the rustic pergola, fairy lights hung in gay swags amongst the vines. Their lights were as yet unseen, because the last lances of sun were jousting through the olive trees.

We were first there, so Peter said we could help welcome the choir members. With our lack of Italian it was slightly embarrassing. The atmosphere was as starched as the choir's white shirts, a huge setting sun made the faces of arriving guests blush-pink too. In the rose-light their shirts and dresses were the colour of blancmange, and the horn on the old wind-up gramophone appeared to be made of solid gold. We shook hands, and tried to make stilted conversation.

The tables were soon laden with the produce from the orto and Peter and Richard's culinary efforts; huge platters of cooked meats - *prosciutto cotto* and *crudo, speck,* and various types of salami cut into colourful circles, all decorated with melon-moons, translucent in the sunset like sticking-out ears. Great wedges of *pecorino*, the size of which would have made a *contadino* swoon, teetered on the edges of plates. The dogs anticipated fortune...

Flickering shadows from the forty or so guests turned the rough-rendered walls into *dolce latte*. The sun quickly dipped below the horizon and dimness turned to darkness, the tiny lights fought and tugged to take the strain. Soon the light from the open kitchen door helped re-define the terrace. It also illuminated the next course, bowls of steaming pasta were carried down the steps, in decorated ceramic dishes. Scented sprigs of basil bounced on top of the mounds and the warm evening smells melded with the aroma of the hot food and dry earth. Copious quantities of white wine from their own vines was passed in a continuous human chain - this was a serious business, like feeding a Legion who'd just fought a bunch of Vandals.

Only after the choir had eaten and drank for a couple of hours did anyone think of actually singing! The gathering had at last relaxed. They had been made malleable by the mellow warmth and sustenance. An aura of well-being had settled over them like a Handel harmonic. Lounging on the long benches, they now leant across the tables, and against each other, with easy familiarity.

I became aware of a noise in the background. They seemed to be tuning up. There was a hum building from the far end of the table - or was it a summer swarm? Just as the mass was taking shape, it stopped abruptly - there was the sound of spoon, gavelling table. Four business-like raps that increased in volume. The conductor's command for silence was instantly obeyed. A man in a striped-shirt stood up and cleared his throat. This was of course the choir's AGM and we were in Italy, therefore a speech was bound to happen. The head of the choir looked more earnest than the others. He confidently went into a long speech about (I presume) how successful or not the activities of the group had been that year. I was drifting off a bit, when all of a sudden the whole assemblage seemed to focus on our little family...

Yes, the man was definitely saying something like:

"Blaa blaady Signor Owen Blaa-dio,"

Peter nudged me under the table, and whispered: "I think you should stand up - Just show your appreciation, you know..."

So up I stood, I smiled, nodded and took the applause, I didn't have a clue what was going on. I said *"Si, certo*, grazie, grazie!" and sat down again, feeling like I'd done my bit. I thought it was very nice of them to give us such a warm welcome. I could see that even Zappa was looking up at me from under the table, her tail was slapping the leg of the bench and stirring up a fair amount of dust too.

The speech was over so the real purpose of the evening could at last begin, now it really was dark - and there was that hum again.

The murmur started to roll through the night air. It gathered voices like a ball of fluff until we were all wrapped in a fleece of sound. Led by a large bearded guitarist whom our kids named Pavarotti, some of the group stood up. A few interlocked arms or perched with one buttock on the table, or even on a fellow choir member's knee. They sang, casually.

Each voice was offered up and taken away from the sound, at will. It was a freestyle sewing of vocals, like a sonic patchwork quilt. Songs from Bach to the Beatles, an eclectic mix from Carol King to the 'King of Kings', in a perfect harmony of spirit and voice. This was no rehearsal, nor a performance for others to admire. This was singing au natural, barebacked, bare-knuckled stuff, it was raw enjoyment in the dusty warmth of an August night. The hot air hit the back of our lungs with every breath. There were no inhibitions, everyone just let rip.

I don't know whether it was the wine, the company, or general ambiance that made the evening extraordinary – but I've never felt quite the same feeling of elation and being 'in the moment' as during that night of shared song.

The singing and dancing carried on through the night until the early hours and having our children with us helped to ease us into the social mêlée - Meri was twirled around for hours, the dry earth whirling from her sandals, while the old 78's, Trad Jazz, 'Ragtime' and Al Bowlly wound scratchily around. Waves of nostalgia combined with the heady scent of hot bodies, jasmine and ripe figs and the sounds of the Thirties echoed through the olives - It could easily have been a scene from between the wars, even the air was turned sepia by the dusty dancing feet.

And that night, Laurie (maybe because of his brand-new manly voice), was offered a proposal of marriage by a retired spinster teacher!

I found out the next day that I had, in fact, been mistaken all evening for someone else. They had thought I was a visitor from an English choir with the Christian name Owen. Unknown to me, during that speech, I had accepted their invitation to twin my non-existent choir in England with theirs. Peter seemed to find the choral exch-ange very amusing. We had unknowingly succeeded in bridging the cultural divide, where their apple crumble and pig-lard soap had failed.

I wondered afterwards if some choir in Ashby-de-la-Zouch (the other Owen's home town) had been shocked by the surprise arrival of a coach-load of hungry, singing Italians looking for a return feast.

During that summer, we spent many evenings in the garden, chatting with Peter and Richard, enjoying the diverse and fine flavours of the region under their pergola. They shared all that was interesting about the area, and passed on useful tips about where to buy certain things, or who to call for a specific kind of help. One of the most useful bits of advice was how to successfully negotiate a fly curtain, whilst carrying a plate of food! Even now when I pass through one, I can hear Richard's voice saying: " One finger! " - Just stick one finger out in front of you, separate the blinds and twist through... simple, elegant and amazingly effective.

The atmosphere of those evenings was enhanced by early Renaissance music, or the music of the Troubadours. We wallowed in the spicy aromas of night-scented stock and dog. In the distance, the lights of Frontone held the castle captive on its hill. It glowed in the cobalt air. Those mellow, muzzy nights soaked into our subconscious like a herbal, hot-tub ... surely, this is how life could and should be .

Much as I love Gloucestershire, there are far too few evenings in a whole summer that are warm enough to stay outside under the stars, talking or just star-staring into the early hours. This life certainly appealed to both of us....

The 'boys' had an *orto* for vegetables. It was a sloping field of about an acre, reclaimed from nature and organised into neat rows of tomatoes, several types of beans, pumpkins, onions, garlic, peppers, aubergines, melons and much more. Aldo, a local who was well into his eighties, helped cultivate the garden. He woke us up every morning at six when he arrived for work on his motorbike. It was an agreeable arrangement because Aldo sold as many of the fresh vegetables as he could at the local market and the left-over abundance came back to Peter and Richard - there was more than enough for everyone's needs. Also of course, the growing season in Italy is a couple of months longer at each end of the summer than in England, so free food came to the table for most of the year.

The *orto* was not their only garden; in front of our cottage was a small formal garden. It was newly planted with clipped box and lavender hedges lining the gravel paths and cascades of the multi-coloured *Marvel of Peru*, which provided generous quantities of bright flowers. We shared an interest in gardens, as we had just started our own garden in Gloucestershire.

The boys were certainly interested when we said we were going on to stay in the well-known garden at Venzano, later that month. We had heard about Venzano, near Volterra from Patti, a journalist who had just written an article about it. She said how quiet it was, like an oasis, and that it was a secluded bit of Heaven. It sounded so fascinating, we had to go and see for ourselves...

We couldn't decide if the small sign to 'Venzano', at the start of the track, was consciously unpretentious or just plain embarrassed about the state of the track that lay ahead. The long, rough road to the converted monastery traversed endless rolling Tuscan fields. Its huge potholes would have put off all but the most determined and if we hadn't been so intrigued by the thought of what lay ahead, we would probably have turned back.

Unfortunately we were not in a four-wheeled drive, but in our little old Citroën. The dust cloud behind us could have been easily spotted from the hilltown of Volterra, some miles away. However it proved to be well worth the effort, (and the chassis damage!); tucked away at the end of the lane, in the middle of newly ploughed blond earth, Venzano nestled like a refuge for homeless exotic plants and wayward lush vegetation.

Hidden amongst high hedges were several small gardens - numerous secret chambers, each a cultivated garden-room of different plants, as perfectly planned as Sissinghurst. Every small garden sheltered the precious plants from the harsh, desert-like conditions of the Tuscan summer heat, and the healthy fecundity was all watered from its own original Etruscan spring that had, apparently, never dried up; that's nearly three thousand years of continuous squishing and splashing, through all those years of Etruscan kings, Lucumos, the births, the deaths, wars and droughts ... without once running dry.

The spring lay at the end of a walkway at the furthest point from the buildings, and was almost completely obscured by the thick undergrowth. The water-source bubbled up under a stone arch. It was so lichen-encrusted that it looked like the secret source of a great river, and was designed to face and be magically illuminated by the setting sun. The sound of burbling water was the only clue that, by parting the greenery, the spring, its ancient arch and small pool would be revealed.

Along the perimeter of the garden, on the other side of the track, lay the stone buildings of Venzano. Low-slung and humble though they appeared, they had an aura of divinity... if the stones could have made music, it would have had the resonance of a Gregorian chant.

Set around a cobbled courtyard, with the comforting sound of another trickling pond, Don and Lindsey, (the owners) had converted the twelfth-century Augustinian monastery buildings into simple, comfortable dwellings. Each was furnished traditionally with *cotto* tiles, lots of wood and marble, chalky white-wash and high thread-count linen. The exterior stone walls were draped with rustic trellises, thickly festooned with rare climbing plants, dangling ivy and grape vines, green on green. The buildings hugged the lands-cape like terracotta limpets, so glued to the terrain that they could never be wrenched off. There was a quiet dignity about the settlement like a sleeping pilgrim.

It was late August so the massive caterpillar-tracked farm vehicles had already churned the richly cropped fields into furrows of glossy earth. From our bedroom window all that could be seen was a land of pale Naples-yellow with no outstanding features -

a ' Sea of Tranquillity'. Actually, because of the white furnishings inside, it was a fascinating cross between lunar and Sahara. In the bedroom, the oak floor shone and creaked like Sam Browne leather. A muslin mosquito net had been tossed over the metal-framed bed, like a hastily-made tent for a desert campaign. The crisp odour of laundered linen added the finishing touch of *Arabian Nights*. It looked and smelled (in a positive way!), like T.E. Lawrence might have just jumped out of bed as we arrived.

From elsewhere in the garden, beneath a flawless sky, derelict farms could be seen cresting the rolling tumps of ploughed earth. Dotting and dashing along field boundaries, the cypress trees stood sentinel marking the passing of the Etruscan empire (or confederation as it be might called it now). For me however, the strange, barren terrain wasn't depressing or ugly. In fact, after a few days, the emptiness of the vistas induced a kind of calm. It was how I imagine it must be on a long solo voyage, a desert trek or space mission, with little visual reference to focus the mind. The feeling of spaciousness must have appealed very much to its previous inhabitants too, making it easier to meditate or get closer to a mental purity, without any earthly distractions...

The contrast of the garden, with its diverse range of greens, from olive to viridian, and abundant primary colours, was exaggerated in its dramatic impact, by the surrounding monotone landscape. It was like one clip of colour in a black and white film. It felt otherworldly, and more foreign than many farther flung places we've been to.

This was not only a wonderful place aesthetically - for Don and Lindsey, it was their living. They had created a well-known and successful plant nursery out of this isolated spot, even providing plants for the Boboli Gardens in Florence. To make a garden at all in this environment is quite an achievement, let alone a prestigious nursery. It's illegal to use a hose-pipe in the driest part of the year in many parts of Italy, so all the plants were watered daily by hand, which meant laboriously irrigating with a watering-can, filled time after time from the spring.

To one side of the monastery was a larger, magical private garden of dappled shade. Paths intersecting through flower and herb beds. Small plants in pots were nurtured and brought on here. Dense, uncut foliage fell over the walkways - it was hard not to trip over. Placed in amongst the herbage were life-sized, sculpted torsos made of red earthenware... pert-breasted nymphs carrying vessels on their heads, like erotic totems or characters from a Derek Jarman film.

It was very surreal if you happened to be alone there as the sun was setting. At dusk, the hot air was heavy with honeysuckle and datura perfume. The pungent scent attracted humming-bird moths, whose drone completed the already monastic atmosphere.

Lindsey, a botanical illustrator, used many plants from the garden as source material for his fine work, and as I walked past his studio one day, Don popped his head out of a nearby window and said, in his Antipodean accent; " You're a painter aren't you? Come and have a look at this..." He led me past the ceramic figures in the garden, I skipped between the potted seedlings, trying hard again not to knock any over. We entered some old doors at the side of the building and he switched on the light;

"We're in the process of restoring it, with the help of a couple of mates."

This had been the tiny chapel for the monastery. There, on the altar wall, under a sheet of milky polythene, was an old religious fresco.(It resembled a scene from *A Month in the Country* by J.L. Carr, in which a medieval wall-painting is slowly revealed from under layers of plaster).

The room was filled with scaffolding and the ceiling had had recently been re-painted with a chalky ' Piero ' blue. Gilded stars were just being added. Half the stars were golden and half were just pencilled in. It was the creation of a miniature universe. I felt I'd been shown a special secret, like the ' mighty Seas of un-built Space' (Edward Young)

It really was a little bit of Heaven.

Our family video of the stay in Venzano shows Meri engaged in chasing, feeding and actually being a swift, wheeling and flitting around the courtyard. Lindsey is seen busy in the evening, trailing back and forth with watering can in hand. Our painter friend, David, who came on several expeditions with us, is lying on the sofa like a bolshy, bored Byron, palm to forehead, moaning; "it's 'six o'clock somewhere in the World, surely?" waiting listlessly for gin and tonic time.

At the end of our stay, caught on the film is a tremendous storm - thunder, lightening and golf-ball sized hailstones bouncing off the rutted road and quickly turning it into a river with rapids. We spotted a farmer driving his tractor across the opposite field. I filmed, and the camera shook in shock as the lightening literally smashed into the ground right next to him.... Meri said: "I hope he's got rubber tyres," to which Laurie added in his new, deep voice; "... and a rubber head!"

In our quest to see more inspiring Italian gardens, we visited Bomarzo, Villa Lante and many others, but none held the essence of Italy as much as the magnificent *La Foce*, in Tuscany. I had been reading Iris Origo's, *War in Val d'Orcia* to Fiona, whilst we were staying in the Val d'Orcia, and so we decided to track it down.

Like many things in Italy, the opening times are quirky - I think it opened only on a Wednesday afternoon, every second week. We had friends who had come to Tuscany with the hope of seeing it, but as they were only there for one week - and it was the wrong week - they missed it.

Waiting in the beautiful courtyard surrounded by its faded lime-washed buildings, we felt privileged to be there. It was as though we'd passed some kind of test by getting the right hour of the right day. We had expected it to be very busy, and that we would be shepherded around in a long line. Fortunately, however, we had the place to ourselves, and what a treat it was to be given time alone in that haven of heat. The only company was the searing sun of high summer. We seemed to float on the heat-haze through the garden door into a space brimming with the smell of baked lavender and cooked terracotta.The air crackled with the sound of cicadas as though hundreds of plastic combs were being scraped down walls close by. Our senses were ground into a fine powder of strongly-scented herbs by a pestle of pounding heat.

The overwhelming heaviness of the temperature slowed us down. Vision became magnified, it seemed to be a new way of seeing. We were able to notice even the smallest, mundane detail... a tail-less lizard on a russet tile... the spiralling shell of an edible snail... an apricot glow on a pot in shade... the verdigris coating on a hot brass hinge... a leaden weld around an iron railing... the silken sheen on a fallen rose... a vibrant green on a shaded lemon... the warmth of touch on a pinkish stone... the lazy curl of an olive leaf... and the hand-made texture of an ancient brick. It was a mesmerising journey that could have been annotated by environmental artist Richard Long or drawn in *Micrographia* by Robert Hooke when he first was thrilled by the microscopic world.

Iris, already from a privileged background herself had married the wealthy Count Origo and moved to La Foce in 1923. They also acquired the entire valley it sits in. Although they were prosperous and could quite easily have lived a life of leisure somewhere else, they used their financial privilege to noble ends, both working hard to develop La Foce over fifty years, improving both the land and the lot of the local *contadini*. Iris Origo earned more respect by risking her life, helping Resistance fighters and fugative Allied troops, during the Nazi occupation of Italy. Such was her commitment to the well-being of the local population that she stayed in the house until the British forces liberated the Val d'Orcia.

The garden also showed her fortitude. Like Venzano, because of the barren surrounding landscape, the creation of a garden was a victory over adversity. Designed by Cecil Pinsent, the site is divided into small formal areas; there is a rose-garden, a pond, pergolas and various terraces.Large terracotta pots were repaired with metal straps rather than being replaced with new ones, adding to the impression that the garden had matured and survived many frosty winters.

Square-trimmed box hedging and potted lemon trees were spread over the terraced levels, the scent of citrus and thyme adding a lighter note to the hot perfumed air. It was a delicious place to float through. And all the time there were vistas of the valley below and Monte Amiata. The space had a quiet, formalised self-respect, all one would expect from an Italianate garden .

Most importantly, what comes across when visiting La Foce is a feeling of being in a place beyond reality something intangible, atmospheric and metaphysical. Perhaps it's because the garden interacts so much aesthetically with its surroundings, that it creates a heightened awareness beyond the mere physical. It was certainly enhanced for us by our relaxed 'dreamtime' state .

Pinsent designed on a Repton if not a Capability Brown scale, using the topography as an art-form. From the end of the garden is one of the most famous scenes in Tuscany. It is a totally man-made, and yet convincingly natural landscape - Indeed, it's a view that represents the image we probably all have of the perfect vision of Italy and is printed on many book sleeves, travel posters and postcards; a winding *strada bianca* makes a shallow 'W' shape up a hillside. The snaking white road leads the eye into the distance, flanked by carefully placed, and yet natural-looking cypress trees. It's as good as sculpting with the Earth itself as one's medium. It takes a great deal of selfless vision to design a lands-cape that will satisfy future generations more than oneself, and is something to do with leaving one's mark on the surface of the Earth hopefully for future generations to enjoy.

I suppose leaving some evidence of your existence is one of the driving forces behind creativity of any sort, and creating a garden could be seen as making the ultimate 'mark' on Earth for most of us, we may not be able to achieve a Hidcote, Bodnant or Great Dixter, and we are all well aware that our efforts will go dust to dust in a couple of unmaintained weedy years, but for a lot of us there is still a basic need for many to scratch our individuality, personality or tag into where we have pitched up on this planet no matter what the scale of plot we've been designated. To understand the original background motivation for us to want to try our hand at creating a garden abroad, I have to dig through the top-soil of memory to expose the underlying reasons.

We've seen many magnificent and inspiring gardens in England, many of which have tried to recreate a Classical landscape or Elysian ideal, such as Stowe, Stancombe or Stourhead. There are also ones that are much smaller but still have an excitingly foreign quality, like Barbara Hepworth's garden in St. Ives, Cornwall, packed with her monolithic, almost primeval, weathering sculptures and surrounded by palms, where one is constantly serenaded by gulls. It's a modest but magical, sub-tropical space, tucked into what she called ' the pagan triangle of landscape' between St. Ives, St. Just and Penzance.

The first time I experienced a Mediterranean garden was, ironically in North Wales: When I was about ten, I visited Sir Clough Williams-Ellis' fantasy landscape, at Portmeirion. It could be seen as a sort of Italianate theme park but I thought of it as a little *fetta d'Italia* which had landed on the Lleyn Peninsular. I suppose the purpose of a theme park, however ill-used the name might be, is to try to bottle the essential quality of its subject, and therefore make it a more intense experience.

Here, what was bottled was a distillation of the Mediterranean. Some of the buildings were reconstructed stone-by-stone on the hillside that slopes down to the sea. Others were built like stage-sets, simply to trick the eye. The whole effect is magical and breathtaking - especially if you happen to catch it on a day with blue skies and few tourists, or if you are fortunate enough to stay in the Hotel there, and enjoy it in peace, when the daytime visitors have left.

Clough Williams-Ellis wanted to prove that "the development of a naturally beautiful site need not lead to its defilement". As an architect he fought against the overwhelming tidal-wave of the Modern Movement and International style - design that was changing the face of many towns, with the dehumanised shopping centres and high-rise flats of post-war Britain. He was regarded as a kind of eccentric rebel by my father who was also an architect and was at that same time busy designing and erecting very modern schools for the baby-boomers of the Fifties and Sixties. Clough Williams-Ellis was, perhaps, ahead of his time, in that he was a self-proclaimed environmentalist and preservationist before the terms were generally recognised.

Although the overall impression of Portmeirion is of Italy, the settlement is not based on any one particular place. In fact there are a huge number of cultures represented, ranging from images of Greek gods to Burmese dancers, but all combining successfully to represent the ideal Mediterranean settlement. Some of the structures themselves are tongue-in-cheek ; there is a scaled-down Georgian facade which transforms a one-storey bungalow into a stately home, and a grand-looking colonnade that actually came from a bombed-out bath-house in Bristol. Another eighteenth century colonnade was carefully moved and rebuilt, stone by stone, from Hooton Hall in Cheshire. It's the very juxtaposition of different architectural styles that turns the conventional into the fantastical. (These idiosyncratic pieces of architecture would probably have decayed and disappeared if they hadn't been reconstructed at Portmeirion.)

There are wonderful piazzas set amongst the buildings, deliberately designed on a human scale, and replicating the atmosphere of Italian communal meeting places. These areas rest the mind and body. Surrounded by palms, terracotta pots and pastel shades of plaster, these spaces are so restful that to get up and carry on down to the harbour can feel like quite a challenge.

As you walk down the steep path to the sea, you pass yet more painted cottages, villas and plants from exotic climes. If it is warm as it was for us, it's very easy to persuade yourself that you're in a seaside town on the Adriatic rather than in North Wales - on down to the shoreline and to the wonderfully theatrical climax; there, moored to the harbour wall, is a fake concrete boat! To put to sea would also be a fantasy.

It's hard not to succumb to this place of dreams.

Portmeirion's dreamlike quality was used in the cult TV programme *The Prisoner*, filmed in 1966/7. Coincidently, some time ago, one of my paintings happened to win a prize in a watercolour competition and was bought by the couple who ran the fanclub for 'The Prisoner' (6 of 1 Club). The prize was a painting trip to Lake Como, Italy, and strangely, as I entered the lobby of the hotel, *The Prisoner* was playing on the television - dubbed into Italian!

We came across another Italian gem by accident even further away, whilst exhibiting in Boston, Massachusetts. We were just killing time before flying home and wandered into what we thought was a private art-gallery. We assumed it would be similar to the Frick collection in New York - a private collection of paintings in galleried rooms, so it came as a surprise to find this was more than a mere gallery this was the perfect recreation of an Italian Palazzo, made by a Bostonian lady, Isabella Stewart-Gardner, in the 1890's.

The house looked quite unspectacular from the outside, but once inside one is transported to far-off Italy . The courtyard garden is a convincing re-construction of the Italian Renaissance; the whole quadrant is filled with the sound of dripping water and wreathed in greenery, adorned with classical statuary and pinpointed with oranges. It is as overwhelming as a bucket-full of basil or climaxing aria if you happen upon it on a dull day in March.

The windows of the palazzo look into the courtyard and so it can be seen from every room, offering tantilising glimpses of luxuriant green. Wandering from room to room, there is also the constant background noise of water, splashing from the fountains and splattering onto stone ornaments - the sounds of a Roman bath house. This 'water-music' echoes throughout the house, cutting out the noise of modern life outside, that would ruin the illusion. The decor of the rooms sits easily with the collection, with their ancient wood panelling and floors that squeak with layers and years of polish. The aroma of age and the feeling of antiquity actually encourages one to respond more respectfully to the art, involuntarily reducing the voice to a whisper: It's a temple built to worship Art, containing many precious treasures, such as Botticelli's *Lucretia* (still considered the finest piece of art in town). There are also Titian's *Europa*, a Vermeer and a Rembrandt self-portrait. The collection contains more than 2,500 artifacts - paintings, drawings, tapestries and ceramics. The venture, both the house and the art was originally inspired by an interest Ms. Stewart-Gardner developed in Italian art history, after she had simply attended a lecture in Boston on Dante.

This Palazzo could easily have been owned by a Montefeltro or a Medici, each room is packed with such exquisitely chosen paintings and artifacts, making it a unique mix that would be difficult to achieve in a public gallery or museum. It has the feel of other idiosyncratic, private collections, like Charles Paget Wade's, at Snowshill Manor, Gloucestershire or Oxford's Pitt Rivers museum. They all reflect personal passions that were indulged and supported by ample wealth. (Interestingly, most of the treasures were acquired through Bernard Berenson, whose garden at Villa I Tatti, in Florence, was also designed by English architect, Cecil Pinsent (the designer of La Foce) - a tenuous Italian link, thousands of miles apart.

So, Wales and then the States; at least the next influence was actually from the Mediterranean, but in France rather than Italy. Being here at the moment in a very soggy Italy, it's quite hard to stay focussed on what really motivated us to want to create a Mediterranean garden. Probably one of our biggest influences of the exotic, in both horticultural and in lifestyle terms, was our annual visit to the South of France; a fortuitous by-product of painting is sharing one's passion with others. It's possible to form an intimate bond with someone who has a painting you've created - they own a small part of you, after all, and may look at it daily. The mutual appreciation or sharing of this vision transcends social boundaries, and can open doors into fascinating places; We stayed with the

Nivens for some fifteen years in the luxurious, pink palace called 'Lo Scoglietto' (an Italian name meaning ' little rocks '), at Saint-Jean-Cap-Ferrat.

It started when Fiona had just had an exhibition at the Medici Galleries in London. Normally you never get to know who's bought your paintings - galleries tend to be cagey about that kind of information .

However, on this occasion, the actor David Niven had breezed into the exhibition and bought seven of Fiona's paintings and had insisted on having some way of contacting her. Then we had a card from him, saying that he had "one foot on Concorde and the other on a banana peel!" He went on to say that he loved the paintings, and was a "big fan"! ... and would like to meet up

Fiona was commissioned to illustrate a book of David Niven's daughter Kristina's poetry, called 'Pour Toi'. So she was invited to Swiss house to discuss details. I was more than happy to tag along. We were particularly financially challenged in those days, having barely enough money to feed ourselves for a week, so mixing with the skiing fraternity of Gstaad was going to be interesting.

For the visit, we had a very small tartan holdall. It was scruffy, partially held together with gaffa tape and not big enough to take both lots of our clothing - let alone our new C&A budget skiing togs. The only thing for it was to wear the entire ski outfits on the journey, moonboots and all. We must have looked quite a sight clumping around Gloucester bus station like spacemen in those over-sized silver snow-boots and salopettes. We caught the bus to Heathrow, not the most glamourous way to start such an adventure. It was a particularly mild - indeed unusually balmy - January day. We got chatting to a guy on the coach who was curious about our outfits, as it was so warm. He was on his way to join the Ballet Rambert in London.

I believed him.

I noticed he kept glancing down at our tatty suitcase, and

looked unconvinced by our story, that we were off to stay with a Hollywood Great. He kept raising one eye-brow and saying;

"Yeah, yeah....oh, really?"

By the end of the journey he was definitely humouring us, and obviously thought we were completely insane. I realised that nothing we could say was going to change that. I glanced back at his relieved face as we got off at the airport. The lady at the check-in at Heathrow was just as bad; she looked us up and down. We were pink and perspiring in all our gear and looked as if we'd just skied down a black run. She took our ticket, saw the destination and with a condescending smirk, asked in a flat, air hostess voice....

"Going skiing, Sir?"

We knew that our finances could be seriously compromised by this trip, as we had well under a hundred pounds in the world and that included the collateral of the suitcase. Having looked up Chateau d'Oeux in Switzerland (where the Nivens wintered), on the map, we knew that getting there could be pretty expensive, especially by taxi. It looked at least an hour's drive.

We worried throughout the flight about whether we would be met and how we would get to the house otherwise. Niven's wife Hjordis had said she would send a car to meet us, so we tried to enjoy the in-flight supper as best we could.

Landing in Geneva the weather was, unbelievably, more balmy than at home. The light drizzle made us look even more pathetic in our ski-wear. However, as good as her word, there was a man holding a little sign with 'Owen' written on it. He had come to meet us... thank goodness.

As we followed him through the terminal and through the doors, I realised he was walking towards the taxi rank - our worst fear:

"Oh no, Fiona, look... it's a taxi", I whispered under my breath.

We got in the back of the big, extremely expensive-looking, white Mercedes taxi - even its rooftop taxi-sign looked top of the range.

It is in fact a good hour and three-quarters journey from the airport at Geneva up the alpine roads to Chateau d'Oeux. We didn't talk much as the driver spoke no English and we thought of our life savings disappearing in one cab ride. The state-of-the-art digital meter was ticking away luridly and we resigned ourselves to penury. The Nivens had booked us into a smart hotel near their house and we drew up at midnight - at last there was a fluttering of snow. To our amazement, there on the Hotel's steps, in a line were all the staff of the Hotel. There were at least fifteen people all smartly turned out and probably there to help us with our luggage. They must have had a shock to see the tartan holdall, but didn't show it. Maybe they thought we were eccentric millionaires or perhaps 'resting' from the stage. One of the porters grabbed the scruffy bag from me and we followed him into the lobby. I tipped the taxi driver and he asked for nothing more, so we were in the clear...

The Hotel manager asked if we were hungry and I just replied that we had: " eaten extremely well on the flight, thank you ". The line of uniformed hotel staff melted discretely into the background, no doubt pretty unimpressed that they had stayed up for us. I think they had been expecting some Pacinos, Powers or Pecks. We were shown to our very comfortable room, the porter dumped our old bag next to the vast wardrobe - probably to make some kind of a point. We then spent half the week wondering if we had to pay for the hotel and when I finally plucked up the courage, to ask the man on reception, he simply said with a wry smile: " It is on Madam Niven's account Sir "; we celebrated with a hot chocolate - each!

The next morning we went up to the Nivens' chalet. A forbidding and very tall butler answered the door, wearing white gloves. We stood on the doorstep looking up at this imposing figure whilst he looked down on us as we stuttered our reason for being there.

"We're here to see, we have been invited... we are expected by Monsieur Niven. " Before we could finish, David Niven, cravatted and suave, gently pushed the butler aside to greet us. He took hold of an arm each and pulled us in from the snow. Hjordis was standing behind him, wearing big fluffy slippers and standing on an equally impressive big fluffy rug, her arms open. They welcomed us warmly, like long lost relations.

"My Darlinks, come in, come in. How divine," Hjordis said, as she brushed some snow off Fiona's cheek.

The hallway looked like part of the set of *What's New Pussy Cat*, dressed as it was with Sixties paraphernalia and everything one would expect; large colourful paintings, great striped animal skins all over the floor (picked up on exotic film locations no doubt) - and lots of curly Sixties stuff. It was a large traditional chalet, all wooden and warm. Each floor had a balcony surrounding it with carved wooden balustrades. There were a couple of rows of balconies nestling under the massive beamed eaves of the snow-laden roof. The land at the back of the house slopped steeply into the snowy valley and towards the picturesque town of Chateau d'Oeux. As we walked from the hall, the vast panorama of the Alps seemed to enter the living area through the French windows.

We went through into the sitting room, full of luxurious sofas, more paintings and a huge roaring fire. The flames hissed and spat behind a great golden peacock fire guard, its metal feathers splayed out to protect the Persian carpets. David took us both by the arms again to give us a tour around the chalet and to show us his favourite pictures (he was a keen painter himself). In the dining room, the sun streamed through the windows, lighting a collection of paintings done by friends and family:

"This one was painted by Hjordis, this one's by Noel Coward...

And this one by a dear, darling friend of ours - Grace." He paused in front of a naive and joyous painting of the room we were standing in, there was the dining table and the picture showed what fun had evidently been had − empty plates, glasses and bottles akimbo. It had been painted by Princess Grace of Monaco who had only recently died in a tragic car accident. It was poignant and there was a real feeling of loss and grief in his voice; it was very evident that a great era in their lives had ended.

There were many extraordinary moments in that week, but one I personally won't forget was losing their car up a mountain. David had taken me ' around the block' - the very snowy block - in his car to show me how to drive it. I'm not sure if I'd ever even driven abroad before - certainly not in a left-hand/four-wheel drive one - let alone it being the Nivens' car. He didn't seem at all worried as I took him for a ride while he showed me all the knobs and dials as we skidded around Chateau D'Oeux, and to distract him from my driving, I told him that when I first met Fiona I had happened to be reading and enjoying his book *The Moon's a Balloon*, which seemed to amuse him. We slithered back to the house. He stood in the thick snow outside the chalet and waived *au revoir* as we headed off up the mountains.

I don't think they noticed but we were gone a very long time. We could have driven back to England in the time we were away. We had parked on the side of a spectacularly snowy mountain and gone for a short walk in the snow to take in the air and fantastic scenery. We didn't get lost the car did. It completely vanished... like a melted snowman.

After literally hours of going round in circles, endlessly retracing our footprints, we started to act illogically; we resorted to looking behind ludicrously small bushes and stumpy, snow-covered fir trees. It was impossible to find. I tried to dream up a plausible excuse for mislaying the car; I had left the handbrake off and it had taken off down a *piste*, or over a cliff or something even more dramatic - you can't just 'mislay' a car. I wondered if this was appropriate for mountain rescue, or even a St. Bernard dog, just for the contents of its barrel but thought better of it. We decided to head back down the mountain as the sun was about to go down. We would just have to face up to our fate; I'd lost their extremely expensive car up an alp, and on our first outing too. How totally incompetent ; they'd been so generous entrusting us with it in the first place.

What was I going to say?

Then, as it was getting dangerously dark and all hope had definitely gone, we stumbled across it, much lower down the mountain than we had thought. It had been teasing us, as though to test our stamina and will. All those alps look the same.

We were exhausted and relieved when we returned to the safety of our hotel room. All we needed was a hot bath and early night. Then the hotel room's phone rang; it was Hjordis, speaking in her strong Swedish accent:

"Darlinks, would you like to come for drinks this evening... with Roger and Luisamaw... yes darlinks, oh good... how divine?!"

Now it's a strange thing with names; if they don't come in the order you expect, sometimes they don't register. So I said: "yes, sure", without realising whom she meant.

So it was a real surprise as we entered the chalet to find Roger Moore standing in the hall. Out of context it just seemed bizarre; he was wearing some kind of all-in-one ski-suit with zig-zags of zips and he looked as though he'd come straight off an action movie set.

Coincidentally, we had just had an exhibition in West Berlin and so when he was introduced to us in the hall as we took our snow boots off, Hjordis said to us, " You were just in Berlin for an exhibition, weren't you ?... Did you meet Roger there - he was filming?".

Fiona said; "Possibly, I can't remember!"

Now she wasn't being deliberately vague, obtuse or cool, actually she really might not have remembered. (Fiona is pretty bad when it comes to any kind of 'film stuff'; we once had drinks with Doreen Hawkins (the widow of Jack Hawkins). All evening, whilst sitting under a large marble bust of the well-known actor, Fiona had thought we were at Stanley Baker's house, whom she had already confused with Stanley Baxter - a triumvirate of errors. Also, earlier that same evening, on the way to Mrs. Hawkins', we had come across Alan Whicker and his partner outside their house. Fiona had said a warm hello, not because she had recognised him, but because she had mistaken his partner for Maggie, a friend in Gloucestershire; he had probably assumed we were fans of his).

Later that evening with the Moores, she made an even bigger faux-pas; Luisa was discussing the merits of various James Bond actors, and turning to Fiona on the sofa asked; "I mean, who do you think of as James Bond - 007?"

Fiona was looking at me quizzically, (I was trying to nod discretely sideways, in the direction of the handsome man sitting next to me, in the very 'Bond-like' jumpsuit), but she still said; "Um, Sean Connery isn't it?"

Another day, when we had returned from a day up a snowy mountain, again very tired, we went to the den in the basement of the chalet where we curled up on the huge cushions to watch a film, while David had a meeting upstairs with his great friend John Mortimer. There was a new-fangled and very large VHS video machine in the den, so I looked through the video drawer and pulled out an old Niven film. It was one we hadn't seen before, called 'A Matter of Life and Death'. The movie was rated one of Barry Norman's top ten films of all time. It was about a dashing WW11 bomber pilot (Nivs), who was about to bail out without a parachute, to certain death. As he talks to the WAAF on his radio he says:

" What's your name ?",

" June," she replies, in that breathy, Forties way.

" I love you June,"

" Why?"

" Because you're Life... and I'm leaving it...."

He jumps, but somehow avoids death because of the thick fog over the Channel, and a huge celestial courtcase occurs; it's a very emotional film and we were both in quite a tearful state as the film ended. Then, through the door, in walked the man himself. A strange time-leap of some forty years - now he's wearing a dressing-gown and slippers and letting the dogs out for a pee! We explained why we were so tearful and he reminisced about making the film; he said they had changed the title, in the States to *A Stairway To Heaven* because they didn't think it would sell, just after the war, with the word 'Death' in the title. He added that the studio had built the longest staircase in history for the film, (no CGI in those days). We said how much we had loved it, and he gave us both a big hug. It was very moving, we felt a linking of his celluloid youth with our youth - film and reality intertwined.

I feel I've digressed a bit, but the whole point of this is to recall the wonderfully exotic garden at Cap Ferrat, which was the Nivens' summer residence in the South of France, and how it influenced and inspired us.

For many years, while our chidren were very young, Cap Ferrat was almost the only place abroad we visited. It became our annual holiday. The contrast with our daily life in Gloucestershire was always interesting. One year, as we waited for our cottage to be renovated, and were living in a tiny (6' x 4') garden shed, we still went on holiday to the Nivens' house with its butler-bell ringing, truffle-guzzling, champagne-pool spoilt-ness! David and Hjordis really were the most generous people one could ever wish to meet. I think they must have liked having us around because we were young and enthusiastic about things. Hjordis often used to say that she saw it all through fresh eyes when we sat on the terrace, enthralled by the view over the bay towards Monaco, which she knew so well.

We always enjoyed hearing the tales of Hollywood days, whilst sitting around the pool after long lunches - scandalous little titbits even now too hot to print.

Hjordis told us how she'd gone into 'our' bathroom (the guest bathroom at Lo Scoglietto) and found Larry Olivier, sprawled out naked on the floor "like a lizard", she said; apparently he had succumbed to some mystery illness and David, ever the gentleman, had hired an air ambulance and personally escorted him all the way back to his home in England. I found it very hard not to picture the scene whenever I used the en suite afterwards.

The House itself could have told a tale or two, I'm sure. It had once been owned by an ex-President of France, and also by Charlie Chaplin. It sat pink and proud on the sea front. Easy access to the water was provided by its own private harbour, which overlooked Beaulieu-sur-Mer and Monaco. To one side was a peninsula garden that seemed to float out into the sea.

At night, the lights of the Grand Corniche lit up the mountains opposite, reflecting the lights like twisting party streamers across the sea towards our balcony. We fell asleep to the hot, holiday sounds of music bouncing off the water from the Casinos and summer festas, all along the coast. Should we become peckish in the night, on the dressing table was a constantly refilled bowl of fruit which looked as though it had won gold at a village fete. Also, there was always a box of Swiss chocolates that seemed to turn alpine-cold as they melted in the mouth. Either side of the four-poster bed were line-drawings of figures, (which had been drawn in a single continuous line, without removing pencil from paper) sketched and signed; "for David", by Jean Cocteau.

From the French doors of Lo Scoglietto leading into the garden, there was a generous, shallow semi-circle of steps. Descending between two larger-than-life, raku-glazed ceramic greyhounds, sitting guard at the top of the steps, a bending path wended its way intriguingly out of sight. Bright-green lawns of spiky Californian grass stretched out on either side of the path and every few yards an elegant olive tree was placed in the grass, Japanese in its casual precision.

Each tree spread out leggy and fawn-like from a bed of bright annuals - busy lizzies, pelargoniums or petunias. To create floral height, plumbago and bougainvillea plants scrambled up the trunks, their pale peach, pink and blue flowers just visible against the smoky bark and glaucous-green foliage. The path unfurled like the spiralling rings around a conch-shell. Quite soon, excitingly, the sea became visible and audible on both sides. It vigorously caressed the garden... suddenly nurture was over ridden by Nature, as the water hurled itself against the besieged rocks even on the calmest days, as though determined to recapture this treasure. The peninsula eased the garden into the constant warm breeze and steady rhythm of the Mer d'Azur.

Around the first bend in the path and just visible through the trees, was what looked like a ruin. The folly could have been taken from a Rex Whistler frieze or a classical landscape by Claude. Only at the climax of the path did the whole folly or Rotunda become visible. Built as a Greek-style architectural folly, it was the perfect full stop. Underneath the circular pillared building was a shower room and small lobby with a fridge, always stocked with Champagne - the perfect refreshment after such a taxing walk (actually it was probably only about 150 metres!).

At the end of the promontory, you almost felt afloat with the sea slapping the rocks on three sides - here, pines arched over the path in elegant contortions and the sea glowed turquoise through the tracery of their scaly branches. There was always the overwhelming scent of pine, salt-sea and Hjordis' perfume; Coco Chanel. Looking back along the path it was possible to see a waving dash of pink, as if the house was still trying to get one's attention through the olive leaves.

The swimming pool was as perfect as a painter's vision, with its Alma Tadema curving marble, squiggled lines and Hockney blues. Surrounding the pool was a large terrace, mottled with holes of light under the olive trees and paved with travertine marble. The area was significant to us because it was where Meri walked her very first steps on her first birthday. A garden so simple in design and yet so utterly beautiful is bound to have a deep effect on you mentally, like a Haiku. It was a 'dream-catcher' garden, not only because it was so dreamlike, but also because the way it protruded into the sea seemed to be luring human aspirations onto its rocks like a Mermaid with a Siren.

Even now, although I no longer have access to it physically, it is a place I go to sometimes, just before sleep, like revisiting an old friend in a very posh nursing home. In a way I still have a mental key to let me into that garden, and it will always be there to make my synapses fizz like the bubbly.

One of the over-riding perfumes that mentally associates us as a family with Lo Scoglietto was the scent of lilies. We had an ongoing joke that whenever Fi smelt lilies at home, Hjordis would telephone as though they were communicating telepathically. At 5 o'clock one Christmas Eve Laurie came running downstairs, he said, "I've just smelt Hjordis' lilies on the landing" ... this time she didn't phone. We found out a few days later it had been exactly the time that Hjordis had died in Switzerland.

The house was full of beautiful things, including paintings; in the library, where one could flick through all the books of stills from the Niven films and his Oscar (for the film 'Separate Tables') sat on top of the TV there was one thing I particularly enjoyed looking at; a small nude painted by Derain.

A few years after our visits to Lo Scoglietto had come to an end, I was reading Peter Ustinov's autobiography and came across a mention of this very painting - apparently Ustinov had actually owned it first. During the Second World War, when both were in the army, Ustinov was Niven's batman and they were living at the Ritz Hotel. Because of the expensive life-style, Ustinov became a bit short of cash, So he had to sell the Derain through an auction house. By chance, it was Niven who bought it, without knowing where it had come from, and so it ended up in Cap Ferrat. I wonder where it is now? One of the amazing things about works of art is that they can have as varied a history as a coin - a story that can run through generations of ownership.

(As for the book, ' Pour Toi', originally commissioned by David, it was eventually launched in the Medici Society's Grafton Street gallery in London, an event attended by a potpourri of Hollywood greats)

We could have gone on soaking up the influences from other cultures as a passer-by, forever without any desire to own a small part of a 'foreign field'. For some, this travel might be the inspiration behind a collection of artifacts, or maybe the spur to make them explore more, each time farther afield, or for some it might lead to them moving lock, stock and barrel to another culture.

For us, these experiences did seem to be leading somewhere too. We started seriously thinking about spending more time painting in another place - finding a second studio, and hopefully somewhere with a warmer climate to create a Mediterranean garden, somewhere to grow an olive tree was becoming a pull of gravitational proportions. We were just waiting for something to motivate us enough, to make us take that big step of committing to a new project.

Was it time to put a stop to flirting with Italy, and do something about it - perhaps we were ready to put down physical roots, get our hands dirty in foreign soil and plant that olive tree?

ROOTS AND SHOOTS

There is a period around ones mid-forties when you look for new challenges; it's a time to see what, if anything, has been achieved in life, - maybe there is just about enough energy left to do something about unfulfilled ambitions. There is a need to re-evaluate, to stand back and take a good look at what can be improved. For some this a real mid-life crisis and for others it might be easily solved by changing the type of car they drive. Or perhaps altering their nose, chin, boobs, wife or husband - maybe even to swop with the one next-door, (only the latter obviously).

For us too, an adventure was needed as a distraction. Our young were definitely teetering in the doorway of our nesting-box. We could see their silhouettes against the hole, even if they hadn't quite flown. It seemed right to fill the gap with something positive.

As they started new lives, so could we...

Painting is, and always has been, our main focus in life, so that would be at the centre of any venture, from which everything else would radiate. Painting is far more than just our income; it is the thing we both enjoy doing most of all in life. An advantage of both of us being painters was that it was feasible for us to be able to live and work in two places, and take our work with us.

Gardening has been the other passion that has run along parallel lines with painting, in terms of both work and pleasure; our garden, which we open along with our annual exhibition at the Old Chapel, (our home in Gloucestershire) has been a huge personal challenge for many years but it has now reached a stage that is more about maintenance than creativity. The Wesleyan, Methodist chapel, dating from 1857, sits on the south-facing side of a deep valley, one of the five valleys emanating from Stroud, and the area developed from the sixteenth century as a centre of the woollen industry.

The various names for the woolen cloth read like a paint colour chart; Stroudwater Scarlet (for military uniforms to run the British Empire), green baize (for snooker tables) and hunting Pink were all made in these valleys, so famed was the fabric that even a tribe of North American indigenous people still call their wrap around shawl a 'Stroud'. The racks of drying, dyed cloth on south-facing slopes of the valleys must have made a festive welcome to the Stroud valleys as one journeyed along the canal.

The solid stone chapel was built half way up the valley side; we wondered for years why the builders had made the extra effort of dragging all the stone uphill? We thought that maybe it was something to do with being able to catch the sun through its large east and west windows when it's at its lowest point at the winter equinox, but then we discovered that John Wesley had apparently preached from the steps here, and so the chapel was built on the same spot.

We began creating the garden in the late 1980's and it was a difficult site for any kind of garden. It was laid out on four different levels with a forty-foot cliff cutting it in half; within the land's boundaries there was no way to go between the levels.

When we bought the old chapel there was no garden at all, just a many-tiered piece of land that was dense with brambles and saplings. Although it was a chapel, there were no graves on the land (not that we would have minded much if there had been, we would have worked around them).

Anything we did with this overgrown acre was going to be an improvement; it was the archetypal blank sheet of water-colour paper (in those days, we didn't paint in oils !)

Fiona, who is the gardener planned it from the outset, I'm more builder/odd-job man. Firstly it was to be Gothic in its intrinsic design like the chapel. Secondly it was to be an allegorical 'Journey through Life'.

This 'Journey' started with Birth as you entered the lower gate and Death as you passed through the top gate... to paradise (or Chalford Hill at the very least!) It certainly made the whole process more interesting, having some kind of plan. Laying paths and steps gave an instant structure too. On the way through the garden one passed various plantings in borders which represented different phases of life: firstly the 'soul border' (soft ethereal colours). Then on to 'the heart' border and below that the vegetable garden. This area had vegetables surrounded by warm coloured poppies and marigolds and divided into four sections with a small formal box hedge surrounding each one, mainly to keep out the badgers. We placed a large ceramic pot in the middle bed and each of the four grass paths is approached through a Gothic-shaped rose arch. This *potager* represented the basic needs of daily life on the metaphysical journey.

That was the first level of the garden. Steep steps then lead up to the next level. ' Onward and upward ' both physically and metaphorically speaking, into adulthood, where a dividing path represented the choices one can make: one option passing through the orchard, which represented the fruitfulnesss of family life, whilst the other path lead to the pond and meditation house - which represented the inner or spiritual life. Up even more steps to the top layer, symbolising the wisdom of later life, where the billowing borders suggest the flowering of wisdom in old age.

The small tower or folly that I built at the end of the top path (twice actually - it fell down the first time), was supposed to look bigger from a distance than it really was, and was inspired by Portmeirion. We sit on top of it at the end of the day and enjoy the sunset up the Golden valley towards Stroud.

Or journeying along the valley and rising up to the edge of the Cotswold escarpment, one can see the more panoramic view over the Severn Vale and even see the distant Black Mountains of Wales.

The Chalford valley nurtured the Arts and Crafts movement; Gimson and the Barnsley brothers lived up the valley in Sapperton as did Norman Jewson, and in the building just below the Old Chapel, Peter (van der) Waals created many fine pieces of furniture. And like a tricky dovetail joint, our land at the Chapel wasn't easy to join together being on so many levels. Logistically it was an impossible site for a garden - the steps alone, which linked the upper and lower garden, via the forty-foot cliff, took a couple of years to build. (If I had known then that other people were going to tread them, I might have tried harder!) Also there is no vehicular access to the lower garden, which turned every small task into a " Sisyphean labour of love " (as a journalist once described it). Like us, King Sisyphus had been cursed to roll a huge bolder uphill for eternity, only to watch it roll back to the bottom each time. I certainly know the feeling... Not even a wheelbarrow could travel between the levels, so everything, tons of gravel and stone, had to be carried on my shoulders. The terrain trained the memory too - any tool needed at the top of the garden, but left forgotten in the shed on the bottom level, meant another energy-sapping climb. It was vital to remember everything needed for any particular job.

After Mary Keen, 'The Independent' newspaper's garden correspondent, visited the garden out of curiosity, and she told photographer Andrew Lawson about it, the garden was featured in diverse publications. It was an unexpected and ample reward for all the effort we'd put in and the spin-off from the publicity was that more people came to see our paintings.

The garden was created purely to have somewhere pleasant to spend time in, drawing and painting, but now after twenty or so years it is complete, and apart from the "big push" of primping and weeding just before the annual exhibition it more or less looks after itself.

So there was physically enough room for a new project.

It was Meri who insisted we seriously looked in Italy. Although it had obviously always been our dream, we had thought that it would realistically be out of our reach. We might have to settle for somewhere that just felt a bit like Italy. Hopefully, not as far north as Portmeirion.

"Just promise me you'll look," she said, as I sat at the computer and she went off to college. So really, I looked up a house-buying website in Italy to please her and so that I could tell her, yes I'd looked but I had been correct it was too pricey.

I came across a website called IHS - Italian Houses for Sale. It was a site in English, directed towards someone like me just playing with the idea of a place in Le Marche. Within minutes of this game I'd seen something interesting… It took me by surprise. I called Fiona down from the studio. She agreed that it looked good. The description of the house made it seem quite ordinary but at least it was within our budget.

Then we saw a photo of the view; what a view, it went on forever - and the house was called *Casa Delle Colline Verdi* the 'House of the Green Hills'. The romance of the name and the landscape around it was too much to resist.

Why was it the only property that didn't have a proper photograph of the house on the website - only the view? The house was probably hideous, but with a view like that it was still worth looking into...

There was no point in dilly-dallying, so I phoned the estate agent in Italy immediately. I felt I was being blown along by a sudden gust of fate.

That was on a very dull Thursday in March.

The following Tuesday we were on a flight to Ancona.

Excited ... *Eccitato*.......... too much excitement!

The thrill of the pre-dawn dash to London's Stansted airport, driving through the dank darkness into an adventure was not only exciting, it was also rather daunting. We sat in the car, silently plagued by trepidations. What had we put into motion?

Even the routine of check in and the safety-mime on the plane, did nothing to distract us from the unnerving fact that we could be on a life-changing trip.

This moment seemed to be a clear dividing line, between past and future – both segments became sharply defined. I suppose I was clutching onto memories like a security blanket. Being on that aeroplane to Italy so unexpectedly made me think of all the other times in our past when something trivial had altered our lives' direction. I had barely taken to my seat when my mind mined quickly and deeply into the past.

Quite often it's been the smallest things that have had the biggest affect and made us steer an uncharted course. This time we had set out into the unknown on the quest for a property in Italy due to the random vagaries of a computer keyboard, but in the past it's been a letter, an advert in the newspaper, or a phone call......

Not being tied to regular employment has allowed our "coracle" to be carried by the current, there is no obligation to turn up on a Monday morning, or to be told what to do, or pay for the mistakes of others (nor do you have to stick around to collect a pay cheque, because there's never going to be one). There is no-one to stop you from spinning on the tide of fortune or to help when you drop the paddle in order to pursue a foolish whim.

There are many incidents in life that fill you with this kind of excitement and I suppose if I had to make a 'Richter Scale' of the high points in my life, it would start at the highest level with being present at the birth of my children. At the lower end of the scale - but still pretty thrilling - would be the feeling of anticipation created by the sound of hammering for weeks before Christmas, and then finding an amazing train-set my father had made, under the tree on Christmas Day. In between the two extremes is a table of peaks (the troughs are on another chart). Memories jostle for a higher place; they jump and shout, "me next" - and then another comes along and nudges it out of the way saying; "oy, I was 'ere first!".

It was a phone call that changed the direction of our lives earlier on, and sent us out of London to start a life-time of painting. At that time, we were both heading towards a more stable lifestyle. We were living in Bloomsbury, London University accommodation and Fiona was doing a post-graduate lecturing course at London University and I was getting a portfolio together to apply to the Royal College of Art, the decision of whether to apply was suddenly removed. To my surprise Fiona arrived home early one day. She'd done a 'Reggie Perrin' or 'a Harold' as they call it in Australia, (after Harold Holt, the prime minister who also disappeared from a beach) She'd just walked out of the college library and never looked back.

She'd been sitting in the library of Amersham Art College where she had been doing lecturing practice. Suddenly, she decided that teaching wasn't the life for her. I think someone had mentioned that if she stuck the job for two more years she would get a pension. That made the decision for her - even two more days doing that job was too much. It was a real 'road to Amersham' moment

Suddenly, from being people who studied artists in one leap of faith and with a brush-load of metaphors, we bit the palette and crossed the thin charcoal-line, to become ' painters '. From that moment on, no other way of life would do for us both. We were now happy to starve for our art and on a few occasions nearly did. The career choice was easier for me, because painting was the only thing I do anyway, and I was tired of being a student . We decided to move out of London and start painting, it didn't seem to suit us living in the city. Every opportunity we had, we'd catch the bus to Oxford just to see fields and trees. We left the 'how to start and where to live' to chance - I think we would have gone anywhere.

Then someone who had lived with us in London, phoned; it was the call that set us on our path. He had come across a place for us to rent in Idbury, near Burford, in the rural heart of the Cotswolds. We would have to share the place with an American writer and printer called William Crosby McRae ('Crosby', I have a vague memory that it was either because he was related to the crooner or because his mother was a fan but I don't think we got to know) - anyway he sounded interesting. We borrowed a car and filled the small boot with everything we owned and made the big move to the Cotswolds, to live life as painters.

We took to William immediately, a tall, sandy-haired Californian who "just loved" the Cotswolds. He was a few years older, and definitely wiser, than us, and taught us to see our own country through his extremely astute eyes. He educated us with his strong views of what he considered to be the best things about rural life. With his quirky, witty way of storytelling, we just laughed and laughed, and started painting. I was instantly enthralled by the rawness of the countryside, the phone call had sent us to the right place to light the flame of creativity.

That winter in Idbury, in what turned out to be the 'winter of discontent', was very.... very cold. The only heating in the whole house was an old Rayburn coal fired range in the kitchen, that for most of the time we couldn't afford to run. So we wore all our clothes at once. William's mother, on hearing about the strikes in Britain on the Californian TV news, offered to send food-parcels. William refused them but we would have happily accepted. I think he thought we looked well fed because of our thick layers of clothes.

We felt justified that we had made the right choice in leaving further education and London - The water-colours seemed to arrive on the Fabriano paper effortlessly, it was as though we'd found the source of inspiration we had been waiting for in life. Committing ourselves fully to this extreme way of living made all the difference; we were no longer people who did a bit of painting in between college work... we were Artists. Fortunately, the very first painting I did, of a view out of the kitchen window (of the farm stockman, Ken amongst his cows) won a prize in an international water-colour competition, and it was just the encouragement we needed.

The view from the spare bedroom window that was supposed to be our studio (but so cold we never used it), remained a total 'white-out' for the first three months - We did not see beyond the road outside the house because of the relentless mist and snow.

From the kitchen-cum-sitting-cum-everything-room, was a sight one probably wouldn't see these days. The mud-filled yard was surrounded by an ancient pillared cattle byre. Its stone-tiled roof, which for most of the year would have been covered in a green lichen cultured like mold from the damp animals, was now iced in ripples of snow, icicles growing day by day. Cattle stood knee deep in mud and their own muck, snow gathering in dirty clumps where their coat was thickest. The rising steam filled the shadows under the eaves, it came from breath, flesh and excrement and was as powerfully animal as Ted Hughes' poem ' Bull Moses '. It was a low, three-sided structure and provided only just enough shelter from the icy north wind to prevent the poor beasts from freezing to death.

Now most of those old cow byres have been converted into luxury dwellings for commuters to Oxford or London. We witnessed it at the very end of hundreds of years of unchanged farming methods. Rural life was still harsh in the Cotswolds. Freezing winter weather dominated everything, snow closed minor roads for days (hard to believe now, but a snow bound week or more was not uncommon then) - it was normal to be cut off. Rural cottages could be forced to survive on in-house rations until conditions improved. Planning for warmth and sustenance was taken very seriously, staying warm filled our thoughts and conversation every day. We painted by leaning our work on the old pine table right next to the Rayburn that we tried to keep alight by scouring the bottom of the coal bunker, and not knowing about such antiquated means of procuring heat once we tried to lubricate its vents and valves with washing up liquid – a big mistake!

At that time we had no car, not because we were trying to live in the past but because we couldn't afford one. So we cycled (snow permitting), walked or hitched everywhere, except on Wednesdays when we caught the bus to the once-a-week market at Moreton-in-Marsh. On one particular market day we became desperate because we couldn't find enough money for the bus fare (it was about 20 pence return).

We looked through old clothes and down the back of the sofa, under mattresses (just on the off chance) and even raised a floor-board when we saw something that looked like a ten pence glinting through the crack - it wasn't. There was no way to scavenge enough money for the fare, so we had to suffer the real ignominy of borrowing money from Dorothy, next door.

William was better off than us - he had a job as a printer in Witney, specialising in American letterpress machines. Sometimes, as a treat and to get us out of the house he would take us for wild jaunts in his battered old Morris Minor, he'd howl like a Californian coyote, inconruously trapped in an English winter - wearing a balaclava and fingerless mittens.

We sped over thick snow to distant pubs that he thought were "really Cotswold ". In those days there really were quite a few unspoiled rural pubs, many in people's sitting rooms. They took in the post for the village, or would cut hair ... on Thursday mornings. The sight of a stranger was looked upon with suspicion or even aggression. William seemed to know them all, and being really foreign, he was more easily accepted than people from neighbouring villages. Not that we drank much - Fiona and I would share half a pint, and William in his Pilgrim Father way would be happy with a shandy. Once, Fiona had a small glass of barley wine (egged-on by William) - she was so unused to alcohol that she was up all night being ill.

In the morning, all William had to say was " Gee Fiona, you

know, you don't have to drink to enjoy yourself !"

There were magical moments too. We all shared the utter joy and visual poetry of living in Idbury. The landscape fed our souls even if we were hungry most of the time. Sometimes William would stop in the middle of nowhere on the way back from a pub up on the high snowy roads, as ' wuthering ' as heights could be. switch off the headlights and engine and we'd all pile out of the Morris... stand and stare at the silent frost-clear sky... it would be just us and the hardy sheep staring, black-faced into a Cotswold night. We had no idea there were so many stars: they were like the specks of dust in our empty pantry. Head tilted back my nose hairs froze with every intake of breath. The cold took us back to imagined hard winters of the past, it felt real and how the season should be and because we'd only just left London it was all the more elemental. It was as though we'd harnessed a force of nature and gained a secret that belonged to a privileged few. The gaining of this knowledge had a deep influence on both our paintings, I think it helped us paint with more gravitas.

They say of Cotswold folk that the " stone is in their blood ", it certainly was bedding its way into ours. We'd go on long walks along stoney paths, over stoney ridges or across iced-fields of Cotswold brash (stone) with only a low stone wall to shelter us from the scything winds. Places where the wintry peace was only broken by the crack of a brittle twig under-foot, or the raging of rooks in naked Elms. The haunting caw of corvids was the soundtrack to that season, although maybe it should have been the Stones.

William shared with us his enthusiasm for forgotten tumble-down cottages that he rated architecturally. He was in touch with a bygone rural age as though he was being channelled psychically by ancient scarecrows. The buildings often weren't perfect... he might take us to see an old hovel with a corrugated iron roof to point out a special stone mullioned window. Or another building with a stone roof that he rated because of its one, huge 'Queen' tile . His knowledge of our land was many layered and totally absorbing, and his fear of what the future might bring was on a par with John

Clare or Francis Kilvert. He'd take us out on frozen Sunday afternoons to tea and cakes in Stow-on-the-Wold. We'd skid in our summer shoes across the icy square to one of his favourite tearooms where he was in love with the prim, very English waitress. We saw our countryside with a foreigner's clarity, and it helped us to define what we, too, loved most about England.

We shared the zenith of a time when our part of the countryside still lay on Laurie Lee's side of the rustic fence. The roads were very quiet and the country was still filled with people who had memories from before what they just called ' The First War'. Edward Thomas' Adlestrop was just up the road, adding a poignant reminder of that war every time I saw the road-sign or heard the distant birdsong of Oxfordshire and Gloucestershire.

Some men still wore breeches tucked into long socks like puttees, and leather jerkins. Some still had pocket watches on chains attached to their rough waistcoats. Almost like a uniform they wore flat tweed caps and mud-brown coats bound at the waist with bailer-twine "to keep the weather out".

These men from a Victorian age were still tied to tithe cottages yet they would spend evenings indoors watching Bob Monkhouse on their rented, colour televisions and would add fizz to their pop with a 'Soda Stream'. It was a transition time from dun fustian to beige Bri-nylon and it sparked with static... lighting a crossroads where old and new merged. Only a few people like William recognised its uniqueness at the time, and he helped us to see it too. He was passionate about stripped pine, rush chairs and rush matting, willow, Cotswold stone, rural accents, marmalade (he thought it was pronounced marmelard!), scones with tea, upper-class people, paintings by Victorian water-colourists (especially George S. Elgood and Helen Allingham) ... and drumming.

William was a drummer without a drum kit; unfortunately, he did own some sticks. You knew when he was home. There was a continuous: tap, tappydetap... tap. Wherever he was in the house, he made his rhythmical presence known; it was tap, tap up the wall, down the stair-rail... on the sofa, along the back of the pine chairs... onto the pine table in the kitchen, t' tap on the Rayburn, on the bags of pigeon feed by the old telephone... on the telephone too, as he passed by... back up the stair-rail and then on each stair, t' tap upwards... on the loo seat and cistern, (how could he drum and pee, at the same time?).

However his greatest love, above all else (even the waitress) were his pigeons. They lived right next to the house in a shed that was a small palace compared to our accommodation. They were plump-breasted, cooing, spoilt things (I think they looked down on us as much as the Nivens' butler). These weren't just ordinary homing pigeons, these were ' tumblers ' - something we'd never heard of, although Darwin had apparently recognised their individual genetic value a hundred years before. They were as bonkers as their owner.

At the crack of another frosty dawn there would be the loud crash of a bin-lid on the roof above our heads... while we were still sleeping. It was the subtle method William used to persuade the birds to get into the air from their cosy shed. The birds would fly in close formation, like fat Red Arrows. Then, shockingly the first time you saw it - one of them would make an ungainly twist of its wings, stall... and start rolling earthwards as if shot down. This quirk had been inbred until the elite would tumble more daringly than all the others, just pulling out of the dive in time to save itself. It was the pigeon equivalent of playing chicken! This was a prize - winning trait and William had many cup winners amongst his team, but occasionally even these aeronautical teasers would get it wrong and hit the ground like a Kamikaze pilot. We would get a silent, drum-free day on these sad occasions.

Idbury was still a place set in feudal times. Ken, the stockman for the local manor, lived next door with his wife Dorothy, in a tied cottage. They had hardly ever been as far as Cheltenham, twenty or so miles away. He told us that when the Second World War broke out, he and his mates went to join up, but when they got to the A40 road none of them knew the way to London.

William had a fantastic old vinyl recording of Cotswold

voices - recordings dating back to early in the twentieth century. We used to sit by the Rayburn on a Sunday afternoon in stitches of laughter hearing the tales of Shepherd Tidmarsh, who had a gap between his front teeth which was 'purrfeck' for castrating the 'sheeps'. Simple pleasures!

Sitting on the sofa listening to the crackly recording, William in his Fair Isle tank-top and flares, would throw back his head and guffaw. He'd gleefully rub his hands between his knees and then suddenly let out another insane shriek of laughter. Then he'd once more sit bolt upright, neck stretching forwards. He'd stay dead still in this strained position for several minutes, concentrating and waiting for the next punch-line on the record...

With torso leaning forward and his pale eyes staring vacantly into space, he really did look like one of his pigeons!

Eventually we had to come to terms with the fact that, fun though it was living with William, we really couldn't afford the very cheap rent. William's sister was living in a rent-free cottage, in return for gardening for a few hours a week, on John Entwhistle's (bass guitarist with *The Who*) large estate, outside Stow-on-the-Wold; " living rent free " - that sounded like a good idea.

We had been in a state of near poverty for a year. We had to find a way of supporting ourselves whilst we painted for our first exhibition. Finding out that there was a network of places to live in Britain where you could work, gardening or cleaning instead of paying rent was the biggest factor in our survival as painters.

Meanwhile on the aeroplane, I'd become so completely involved in this trip down a memory cul-de-sac that I hadn't noticed, the air-stewardess standing in the aisle next to me - she seemed to be waving at my privates.

"Excuse me sir", she said, still gesticulating ," I can't see if your safety belt is done up?'

"Oh, sorry... I was miles away, yes it is actually." I held my jacket up, like an obedient child showing clean hands to teacher.

The engines were running, and we'd started to taxi; how ungainly the rattling mass of plastic and metal seemed as it jolted over joins in the runway, not in its preferred environment, I thought. For me, too, the environment of the here and now was not as appealing or as comforting as the past.

Having answered an advert in the *The Lady* magazine, we agreed to live in an attic flat, part of a Georgian house near the river Severn. The countryside here in the vale was cosy, mellow and tame compared with on the top of the Cotswolds. The hamlet we were to move to was cut off for part of every year by the flooding Severn, making it a real backwater. Although we were still in the same county, we could have been in another country. Gone was the cold Cots-wold stone which turned each village prematurely grey. Here, there were half-timbered, red-bricked buildings which seemed to have a patina of heated bronze. A stillness replaced the constant breeze, so the need to be on the move for warmth was substituted by a kind of torpor. Fields looked greener, pollarded willows were bushier, horse chestnut trees spread out more languorously and even the Friesian cows were slow moving and plump.

This was such a mellow place, it was possible to doze off to a lullaby of curlews whilst waiting for the village bus. The birdsong seemed cradled by the vale and was amplified by the thick morning mist and cloying dew. Small work tasks would take hours, as the heavy atmosphere drag-netted the mind. The only really early birds were those out netting elvers pre-dawn or before a Severn bore.

Patience was essential when the river took control of the landscape. Powerless when faced by the rising water, as first edges, then whole roads vanished so quickly - an hour's detour became the norm. Time spread out like the flooding tide, it had a new value. An old man near Tirley, knowing the annual flooding was a constant, didn't sandbag or fight against the inevitable, he simply had a boat tied to the bottom stair rail inside his house all year. When the tide was high, life carried on as normal. 'The Boat' pub at Ashleworth was often a foot deep in water, one simply wore wellington boots and waded to the bar. For the locals, the inconvenience was ignored; it simply slowed life down another gear.

When it wasn't flooded, a stone could be kicked along the main road for a mile, without shimmying for a car. There was no rush - in the lane beside the house the black and white procession of cows swayed with the slow dignity of a New Orleans funeral. The twice-daily milking of the cows was a rhythm that clocked our daylight hours, while Dandelion clocks floated in the still air as though they had abandoned time completely.

The attic flat we moved into was wallpapered in a dense green and there were bars on the windows. It had once been a nursery, and was warm and quite claustrophobic - it was like living inside a lettuce cloche - just looking out at the pasture land from a deep bath through the attic window was as soporific as avena sativa (a herbal sleep potion made from lettuce).

The first dawn, we were woken by an extremely loud, bloodcurdling cry, not just above our heads like William's bin-lid hitting the roof... but just as alarming. It sounded like someone was being done in on the country lane below - we had no idea what it could be. When we got up the puzzle was solved, we opened the curtains to see the magnificent, full-frontal display of a peacock on the adjacent roof. The peacock's cry woke us every morning from then on, like an aristocratic alarm call.

Sometime later, after we'd settled in and picked up our brushes again, the lady we had moved in with, casually mentioned that her daughter-in-law, who lived across the road in the Manor House, was "something to do with publishing". In fact, she happened to be the Director a very large, prestigious art publishing house in London.

Answering that advert in *The Lady* changed our lives more than any other single decision we ever made. Over the subsequent years we both showed many times at the Medici Society Gallery in Grafton Street, London, and they frequently published our paintings as cards and posters. They really looked after us, even giving us breakfast quite often, all through the 80s and 90s. Suddenly, our work was made available to an international audience.

Once, someone came to an exhibition at the Old Chapel, and on seeing one of Fiona's posters said, excitedly: " So you are the artist who painted this?.. I'm a missionary, and I've been buying this from my local trading post in Papua New Guinea !"

Living in rent-free properties was the way forward for us. It released us from the cycle of having to pay rent, so we didn't need to earn as much - we were time rich and readies poor. I was able to get an early morning, part-time job in a bakery and Fiona cleaned the big house, leaving the rest of the day free for painting.

One of the most difficult things about painting as a way of making a living is that, first, you need to give yourself time to create the work before you can have an exhibition. There is an initial period where there is no way of supporting yourself. It is a time of going without things. We were fortunate, because we had never had the luxury of a regular income, so we had nothing much to miss .

Over the next three, long and tiring years, (I never really got used to the bakery hours), I worked in a couple of bakeries. It meant getting up before sun-rise and working in a 'proper' job for long hours before coming back to work as a painter. I always held onto the thought that one day it would be possible to just paint. I only ever saw myself as a part-time baker who was really a painter.

The first bakery was in Gloucester, a fourteen mile round trip, starting at four in the morning. We still had no car so cycling was the only option. I never adjusted to that surge of energy needed to take my unwilling body from sleep to action so early in the day. Once to make life even more challenging the right pedal fell off my bike and I had to cycle all the way there and back just using my left leg! I walked oddly for weeks afterwards...

Eventually, we were given a very old Triumph Herald convertible by my sister, Joy. We didn't fare much better though - it kept breaking down. On one occasion the gear-box became jammed in reverse gear in the centre of Cheltenham. We had to drive all the way home in reverse, about twelve miles - we had the roof down but we didn't look exactly 'sporty' because we were driving backwards and had a car full of picture frames! I tried to wave nonchalantly at a farmer as we reversed down a country lane, at speed. I could see his plough-furrows go wonky as he turned on his tractor seat to make certain of what he'd just seen.

As staff of the big house, we were privy to the ' downstairs ' world. It was a revealing insight into a life we had not experienced before, because sometimes you could be treated as if you didn't exist. Fiona was once handed something by the wife of a retired bishop, who had been staying as a guest - she assumed it was going to be a tip...

" Here girl, take this," the lady said, " I couldn't quite make it to the lavatory." Shockingly, Fiona was handed a large pair of wet knickers - it was as though Fi was so low down the human-life/ society chain she didn't merit any excuse, apology or even a tip!

One evening we were invited to the game-keepers for dinner. As a pre-dinner treat, he walked us up his field to proudly show us a coiled up white tape-worm one of his sheep had just ejected. I had just about recovered from feeling nauseous when we were presented with an over-flowing plate of *tagliatelle* for supper! Actually he and his wife were very kind and when he heard of my job problems he gave me an introduction to his friend who ran the local village bakery. *Comptons* country bakery was only a couple of miles away, which was a big improvement in distance. The only problem was that it was up an almost vertical hill to get there .

Cycling up the steep hill at the start of the journey certainly woke me up and very nearly did for me. It took me until after I'd loaded the bread-van to recover. In this job I was delivering the bread, rather than baking it and I was almost my own boss. How inspiring it was driving the bakery van up over the Malverns at sun-rise. The ribboned hills lay sleepy at that time of day, as though they were still resting on a mattress of undulating mist and the paths and indentations on the hills took the early morning shadows like the surface of a cantaloupe melon.

I may have been in employment but I felt a huge sense of romantic and artistic freedom. At that time I was making a series of paintings of cow's bottoms with numbers on so there was no shortage of subject matter. At every dairy farm along my route the first stirrings of the milkers could be heard and the odour of dairy cleaning fluid and fresh dung filled the air. Alone on by-roads and lanes the van struggled to climb the hills weighed down as it was with steaming loaves and lardy cakes.

I felt so in touch with Elgar as his enigmatic themes pounded through the tape player in those human-less hours, delivering bread to shops he might even have known. How sympathetically the timbre of his music echoed in the swaying bread van as it crossed the Malvern hills. If he'd experienced the heady-bready aromas in that van, I'm sure he would have made room for a "variation" about it.

The various Gloucestershire names for a pound of baked flour and water fascinated me: there were bloomers, tins, cobs, cottages, twists, crowns and fish. I could never quite understand why, if I took the wrong-shaped pound of bread to a shop in Ledbury or Tewkesbury they would be so annoyed. I just thought, for goodness sake it may be a different shape but it's the same amount of cooked dough. I couldn't understand why they didn't see the logic. I suppose my focus was somewhere else. I feel I should apologise to those shops now for having my mind on Elgar and cow's bottoms, instead of the particular shaped loaf they wanted.

Deer, hares and rabbits romped free in the fields of damp dew and through the dark pleated pine forests as I drove passed Eastnor Castle. The smell of dawn is a 'new born' aroma that seems to renew the senses and is only available to the few early-risers as a daily draught. It must be the time of day that most pumps the brain with new ideas and thoughts of the future. Feeling alone on the Planet focuses the mind. I had ample time - a few years - totally alone at that time of day, in which to contemplate my creative direction and wonder if there would ever be a time when I wouldn't have to get up before sunrise.

The old van rolled on as first light coated field and road with a Severn salmon pink. I passed Dymock where Robert Frost, and his poet friends once lived, then on to the floodplain of the River Severn. It felt like I was one of the first to hear the news of the day on the radio too. One morning, I had to pull over to absorb the unconfirmed breaking news from America that John Lennon had just been assassinated.

Driving the bakery van was a great job and Andrew Compton was a benevolent boss, even when I got the orders wrong (which was almost daily). If I was running short of cash he'd try to find extra arty jobs for me to do. He'd ask me to decorate a special cake with pictures made from edible food dyes or even paint the bakery's window frames!

We lived in a couple of other rent-free places over the next few years, but eventually the sleepy old Severn got to us - we needed a faster pace and started to yearn for the hills. Gradually, we moved our way across the vale and rose once more up the escarpment onto the Wolds.... it felt like climbing back up into fresh air.

The last rent-free place was a large Cotswold stone house with six or seven bedrooms, in Nailsworth. We had heard about the empty house from Janet and Brian Davis who ran a little gallery there and were keen to help out young artists. The house was owned by a friend of theirs, a gruff but kindly retired lawyer. He was also an old fashioned patron of the arts and he quietly helped other artists too, but would have been appalled to think they knew what he was doing. We wrote him a cheeky letter saying that we would love to live in his empty house but we couldn't afford to pay any rent! His curiosity was aroused enough by the letter to invite us around to discuss the matter in his home, a Georgian mansion that had once been owned by the politician, Rab Butler. Over glasses of South African sherry we struck a deal that we would do up the house instead of paying rent. We told him that within a year or two we hoped to leave to buy a cottage and he would be able to sell his house.

The plan had only one flaw from our point of view ; when we moved in, we didn't even have the £2.50 to buy some material for Fiona to make a skirt for a part time job at a local catering firm, so how would we ever get the ludicrous amount needed for a cottage? But we didn't worry, and left it in the hands of the Jinns.

Our painter friend David (of the six o'clock gin tantrums in Italy) joined us in the house and for another three years none of us looked up.... we worked continuously often painting right through the night (we sometimes listened to Sheila Tracey's *Trucking Hour*, programme on the radio, I remember). We were working on exhibitions for Bath, London, the Royal Academy Summer Exhibitions and commissions for the Fine-Art Publishers.

The cottage was on the side of a south-facing hill directly above what used to be a pub, called The Shears. It was where the "The Autobiography of a Super-Tramp" poet W.H.Davies used to drink, when he lived up the road in Glendower cottage. We felt a certain empathy with his poetry, as we too had "no time to stand and stare" - We were too busy painting.

We took it in turns to shop and cook. Shopping seemed more leisurely in in the early 80s - those pre-supermarket days - it took most of a morning, going from shop to shop in Nailsworth. There was a nice lady in the butchers, who used to take pity on me, as a man out doing woman's work. (It was during working hours, and so I obviously looked unemployed) - at that time, there were very few men out and about on a weekday. She always gave me extra beef mince.

Eventually, we managed to get a better part-time job than the bakery one (we still couldn't survive on our painting alone) - now we were staff in an outside-catering set-up at the local delicatessen *William's Kitchen* . They did all the royal do's, and smart weddings in the area - royalty is thick on the ground in Gloucestershire! Instead of working in the bakery for £25 for a six-day week, it was suddenly possible to earn £40 in a night, for an all-nighter like a Hunt Ball, which allowed us more time to paint.

We stayed up all night at the balls, and cooked breakfast for the hung-over revellers at dawn. William was the perfect boss; when Fiona and I worked together, he often set aside a little table with left over food and a bottle of wine, just for us - he called us 'Mr & Mrs. Rembrandt' ! He even parcelled-up bits of delicious food for us to take home and wrote on it the "Starving Artists fund".

David and I were the champagne waiters. Sometimes, our hands would be red-raw and blistered from the number of corks we popped - not the kind of job one would normally link with a work-related injury. A couple of tips for people having difficulty opening 'champers', one: hold the cork firmly in one hand and twist the bottle (never try popping the cork with thumbs, unless you don't mind being hit in the eye) two: a waiter's secret that was passed on to us - but I promise we never used - wipe the sweat off your forehead on the top of the bottle to stop it overflowing with fizz, the salt apparently stops it.

It was an enjoyable job despite the blisters, and was almost like being at a wedding party every weekend. Many of those functions in one of Britain's financial boom-times were extremely decadent. What was sometimes spent on floral decorations alone, would have been enough for us to buy a small cottage.

David once commented about a tented function at Buscot Park: "Well, I wouldn't say the marquee was large, but you could see the curvature of the Earth in it".

We were already a quarter of an hour into the flight to Italy, and this memory-jog was proving to be just the right distraction. The take-off had been smooth and as we levelled off and the acceleration dropped a notch, we looked down at the cold water of the English Channel. Only fifteen minutes gone and even though we'd had breakfast at the airport all our sandwiches had been eaten as well - some things never change!

Looking out on a choppy, cloudy sky over Northern France reminded me of a more unstable flight we made to Berlin, twenty-five years earlier…

Life and work had carried on relentlessly in Nailsworth. As months turned into years, we were becoming more and more aware that we had run past our allotted time for living 'rent-free' in the house. The landlord didn't seem to mind but the chance of buying our own cottage still seemed highly unlikely. Then the phone rang and once again our life changed.

" Hello, this is Christies Contemporary Art here, we've had an enquiry from a gallery in Berlin, asking if you could get in touch with them?"

I phoned the gallery in Berlin and arranged to meet one of its Directors in London the following week.

We met Christian Titze, a Director of the Sagert Gallery, West Berlin; he had seen our work at the Bath Contemporary Arts Fair, and wanted to exhibit it in Berlin. They had an unforeseen space in their exhibition schedule and we were offered a show in December - that gave us only four months to complete the paintings. Hard as it is to paint to a deadline, we knew this was too good an opportunity to pass up. We hoped for the muse to come quickly, and shut ourselves away to paint.

We got on well with Christian - he was the son of the gallery owner, and not that much older than us. The Sagert Gallery had been in existence since the 1860s, which was a long time considering Berlin's turbulent history.

Talking of turbulent, we flew out that December in very stormy weather. We came in to land in Berlin, hit the runway, bounced a couple of times, then took off again. The aeroplane suddenly skewed to the left and accelerated. We banked steeply and sirens started hooting. My fingers dug into the arms of the seat and I flicked the lid of the ashtray to distract myself.

I looked out of the window - there was a close up, lopsided view, straight into high-rise Berlin offices. Secretaries oblivious to our drama, were typing as normal. Everything seemed to be happening in slow motion. The scene outside had the voyeuristic detail of an Edward Hopper, all the colours stood out like the new technicolour era of his paintings. We scudded past the illuminated office blocks - the secretaries not even glancing in our direction and completely unaware that they could have a sudden involvement in our flight. Then we dipped and took another sharp left, and suddenly we were bouncing on the runway once more, just another near miss that fortunately didn't make the headlines.

The pilot said sorry, and that it was the stormy conditions... but we were hugely relieved when we landed, and will never know if it really was a close call.

Christian met us, and drove us to his large apartment in the centre of town, where we met his wife Chin and little boy Benny. Chin was Taiwanese and she knew the best places to eat Chinese food in town. We agreed to go out for a meal that night to celebrate our arrival... and survival. Christian's father was to look after Benny at the apartment.

Christian put a video on of 'Fat and Thin' (that's the no-nonsense German name for Laurel and Hardy!) Benny laughed at the slapstick comedy as he unwrapped our little present from England. We shared the same sense of humour, so I knew Christian would think our gift was humorous, too... but it was the first time we'd met Walter, Christian's father. He was very formal and upright for a man in his late seventies, and he was the Big Chief at the gallery so making a good impression was vital.

Benny and I were still fooling around, and had just finished inflating his new toy. The large, inflatable Spitfire was launched by Benny - with quite an impressive force for a three year old.

It took to the air far more smoothly than the plane we'd just landed in - it even seemed to gain a bit of momentum at head height. The aeroplane, accurate in every scaled down detail struck Walter right between the eyes as he came through the door. He emitted a weird kind of noise a bit like a deflating toy, then lowered his head slowly to see what had struck him. He took a good look at the crashed Spitfire at his feet and said coldly, in almost perfect English:

"Ah, yes I remember these very vell..."

" I'm not amused", was written all over his face.

It really wasn't the best of introductions to the managing director of the gallery we were about to exhibit with.

West Berlin was an island in the middle of East Germany, before the Wall came down. Seen from the air at night, it resembled a shining jewel surrounded by a ring of light (the Wall) - beyond was the darkness of East Berlin and the surrounding countryside. It was our first experience of the Eastern bloc. (Later on, we toured around the whole Soviet Union down to Tashkent, Samarkand and Alma Ata and witnessed an even poorer side). The contrast with the West in terms of material wealth, was plain to see .

Christian, as a resident of West Berlin was not allowed to venture into the Eastern side of the City and actually he had no desire to cross to the 'other side' . We couldn't believe his lack of curiosity for what was going on just a mile away, beyond the man-made frontier that separated him from his fellow countrymen. We couldn't wait to see the other side as tourists had only recently been allowed in.

The infamous Checkpoint Charlie was our coach's route into another world. The thick concrete walls were bedecked with razor wire, a harsh contrast to the Christmas decorations on Kurfursten-damm Strasse that we'd just been driving under. Soldiers took aim at us from sentry boxes as barriers were raised. They all seemed to be taking it so seriously, where was their Festive spirit? I found it hard to keep a straight face... but this was no joke. The armed guards took twenty minutes to work their way monotonously through our bus. They checked passports without a smile, then they scoured inside the bus - between the seats without so much as a smirk and even under it with mirrors on long poles and with equally long faces. I wondered what they were looking for ? People running away from the West - unlikely I thought.

We spent the day travelling around the former capital city of the Third Reich, that once was as Christian told us, the largest city in the World, (although maybe one of the three largest accord-cording to Wikipedia!).Shockingly it was still in a semi-ruined bomb-ed out state nearly forty years after the end of the war. It was a bleak, cold day and the drab-looking citizens were hunched against the sleet or the oppressive system. The shrapnel-marked buildings were caked with layers of grime - pallet-knifed on as creamily and thick as a Kyffin Williams' painting. Many buildings had trees growing from their skyline standing stark against a mortuary-marble sky. You can imagine how dreary it was compared with the festively dressed West. By the end of the day, we were thoroughly depressed.

Fortunately there was a glimmer of light at the end of the eastern tunnel... the highlight of our day out was to be the Pergamon Museum: At first it was interesting because it was like the museums of our childhood in the sixties - it was like stepping back in time. There were row upon row of poorly lit artifacts, all crudely displayed in huge glass-fronted, dark wooden display cases, difficult to peer into, with the 40-watt lighting. The nostalgia-trip was beginning to drag, when...

By chance, we came across what was once considered one of the Seven Wonders of the World, (before it was demoted to number eight) and for us it was certainly the wonder of the day. We wandered unknowingly into a large salon that housed the 50ft high Ishtar gate and the Processional Way of Babylon. The walls were covered in bas-relief dragons and aurochs, standing proud and primitive on brilliant blue-tiled walls. Aurochs were like over-sized bulls, (one of the daring sports of the day was to leap over charging aurochs, and it was thought to be the precursor to bull-fighting.) These creatures were of artistic and mythical significance all over the Ancient World, because they adorned the walls of Thera - we've also seen them on the walls of Knossos in Crete and of course a variety bull sports, still take place, from Georgia to Spain.

We were transported back in history to Plato's "Atlantis" - a mythical time of dragons and minotaurs, Jason's voyage up the Black Sea, tales of the Greek Heroes and even Poseidon himself. We were certainly carried away - it had been worth suffering the depressing day, just to see this.

This really was a part of the Walls of Babylon that had hung in our minds like a garden, since our primary school days, and was now hanging out in front of us. So engrossed were we in the monumental structure and enjoying the fix of colour too, that we completely lost track of time. I looked at my watch - we were supposed to meet the bus in only a couple of minutes - but how to get out - where was the exit, there were no signs?

We sprinted down some stairs... too far. We ended up in what seemed to be a basement or an area where they stored exhibits not on display. We ran through corridors like the catacombs with sarcophagi stacked against the walls, lined upright in rows - there were hundreds of them.

All the corridors looked the same. There were no exit signs – evidently graphic design hadn't made it to the East yet. Where were the stairs back up?

Christian had told us to make sure we got the last bus through the check-point or else we'd be arrested and it would be Embassy business to get us out. It really would be like taking part in a spy thriller after all. But, at that moment we were taking part in an Egyptian tomb thriller, instead. Looking back it felt as though I'd turned into 'Indiana Jones' and Fiona was some kind of precurser for 'Lara Croft' - running like lobotomized mummies up one hieroglyph-clad corridor, and down another. We were breathless and on the point of despairing - there was now no doubt that we would soon be meeting the *Stasi (East German Police)* for a chat.

Fiona stopped for a moment to ease a stomach cramp and lent back against a door. Alarmingly and amazingly it opened... suddenly we were at ground level and outside - tossed into the freezing night air. There right in front of us, parked just outside the Museum and revving its engines, was the last bus out of East Berlin. (I know all this sounds a tad implausible and over-dramatic but if you don't believe me ... ask Lara) .

In a moment we were safe and glad to be back in the warmth of the coach. We'd never been so thrilled to see dralon. Oh, the wicked coach-seats of the West !

West Berlin was a place with a unique atmosphere in those

days. It somehow felt illicit and like a frontier-town where extremes were tolerated… It was a decadent island of frivolous fun in the middle of a humourless sea - like a fop at a fundamentalist's funeral. Because of its past, there was a feeling of latent violence in the air. It hadn't been that long since people had been shot for trying to cross the Wall. There was a place in West Berlin you could visit to see photos of the poor unfortunates who hadn't made it to freedom, people shot for trying to climb over a wall. Even in the middle of the city's large lakes there were buoys marking the frontier and reminding West Berlin's bathers where the good times would end. If you swam beyond the buoys you would be picked up quickly by the ever-watchful *Stasi*.

The only thing that couldn't be separated between East and West was the sewage system under the City. Communist and Capitalist crap all mixed together in the ultimate poolitical satire, a kind of a underground excremental harmony! It's probably the best metaphor that humanity could ever have for seeing the bigger picture.

Meanwhile above ground, separation and observation continued … everywhere seemed hazy and slightly unreal, it was as though heavily over-coated spies were always lurking in the dense mist that came up from the bipartisan sewers. I remember one evening as being particularly atmospheric; just before Christmas, we'd had dinner with an American airman who had bought a painting. He and his wife lived in a penthouse apartment overlooking the snow-covered rooftops, facing towards the Wall. A huge and exuberantly lit Christmas tree stood in the attic window like a tantalising talisman for the East to see but not to touch. After dinner, the airman saw us to our cab and stood on the street corner. He looked tall in his air-force greatcoat, its collar pulled up to protect his ears from the bitter cold. His breath mingled with the swirling steam from the drains and the snow made epaulettes on his uniformed shoulders - all it really needed was Anton Karas on his zither and it could have been a scene from *The Third Man*".

The exhibition in Berlin was very exciting - every day, when

Christian came back to the apartment, we seemed to have sold more paintings in the Gallery. Then towards the end our stay, amazingly a convent / hospice bought all the remaining paintings. At last we could fulfil our promise to our landlord and move on.

Christian loved visiting us in the "Cotsvoods". He was fascinated by all the quaint village names around us, but usually pronounced them wrongly.

" Freddie, I am loving the sound of ziss Pin-fartings!"

Which was of course, Pinfarthings.

Eventually he decided that he wanted to set up his own gallery in Berlin; I was driving him back to Heathrow when he asked me, in a very serious tone:

"Freddie, I'm am not knowing vat to call ziss new gallery, do you have any ideas?" (I know this German accent is hard to believe, but he really did talk like this!) Trying to concentrate on the motorway traffic as well, I just suggested off the top of my head: "I don't know - how about the Nailsworth Gallery?".

After a moment's contemplation: " I like ziss !" he said, to my surprise. " I like ziss very much."

So in Potsdammer Strasse, in the heart of West Berlin a new gallery opened - it's smart sign written the English way, read: The Nailsworth Gallery ... shame I hadn't suggested Pinfarthings really !

We were now well into our flight to Ancona. An hour of recollection had passed. I could make out below that the land had started to rise into an Alpine hinterland. A powdering of snow was whitening the mountain tops and the rolling hills seemed to be gaining height below the aeroplane. Within minutes the mountains were under us. It felt like it would be easy to reach out and touch the isolated snowy peaks.

"Any more rubbish, sir?" the steward asked, as he reached for my empty sandwich wrapping, it was as though he could see what I was thinking too. On a flight, one is already in a kind of suspended animation. This is not reality - you're already floating through the implausible. I've never really had faith that a hunk of metal with the addition of a few hundred heavy people can stay up in the air. It's not a sensible train of thought to pursue as a passenger at this stage of a flight, we're only half way through and there are very pointy mountains below. Better to find another distraction…

I remembered another phone call: "This is IPC magazines here; our Director has requested that we get in touch with you. She's is in London next week and would like to meet up ?"

IPC Magazines is one of those international companies that owns and runs many different magazines, both in the USA and the UK, and was originally founded by William Randolph Hearst and D. was a Director.

We met D. and her husband in the Mayfair Hotel, and got on really well over a jolly good tea. They also ran galleries both in Palm Beach, Florida and on Long Island, New York.

(She had come across an article about us in the UK *Country Living* magazine and realised she already owned one of Fiona's paintings which she'd bought from a gallery in Key West, Florida). They offered us exhibitions in both places.

The first time we drove into New York we travelled into the city from the Hamptons in an extremely ostentatious stretched limousine. Within sight of the sky-scrapers of Manhattan and without warning, the limo died. On the main freeway in the outer-lane it simply slowed to a halt, like a fading Gershwin trumpet solo.

There was definitely a vibe of "Tee Hee, that'll serve you right... you flashy bastards!" from the passing commuters as they glared at us and tried not to crash into us. It felt like being one of Lord Raglan's 'picnickers' overlooking the charge of the Light Brigade, with frenetic life rushing on all around. We remained motionless and helpless. Actually I figured that we were ensconced in so much tin that even if something had hit us we'd hardly even feel it. I don't remember feeling worried - we just carried on chatting, small talk passed the time as the maelstrom of hurtling traffic went on outside. I just expected it to be sorted... We didn't have to wait long - in about five minutes, a large cop on an even larger motor-bike pulled up behind us. Like a member of the Thunderbirds family, he took control admirably. First of all he extended a pair of tall telescopic arms with big red stop-lights, from the back of the 'bike. Then, balancing rather precariously considering his size, the NYPD cop appeared to stand on his motorbike's back, feet astride his panniers like a Colossus. He slowly raised his arms and commanded five lanes of traffic to stop. Up there he looked and must have felt like Moses. This man could easily part the waters, I thought. I couldn't believe it... such power he single-handedly stopped the morning 'rush hour' into New York. I could see the vehicles behind us were stopping in orderly waves and very quickly formed a massive static traffic jam. This mesmerised shoal were held in limbo like a great tickled Hudson River Trout. However angry and frustrated the drivers must have been, there wasn't even a single beep. In seconds the density of traffic must have made a grid-lock several miles back and the queue kept doubling in size every few minutes. Wall Street financiers would have to wait... Tribeca artists had to wait... shoppers and shop assistants had to wait... and even uptown thieves and downtown muggers had to wait... until this man gave the off again.

Meanwhile we were shunted ignominiously, firstly onto the hard-shoulder and then down a slip road into Queens. Behind us the cop slowly dismounted like a Duke off his mount. There must have been a little bit of John Wayne tingling in his brain. He had sublime power for those moments and had single-handedly controlled the main route into the one of the most powerful cities the World has ever known. The more I think about that time-lock, the more amazed I am by it - had that policeman held the traffic up for any longer, what might have been the long-term, Gaia effect on the World? - a major financial deal could have gone unsealed… a bank may have folded under the strain… there might even have been a run on the bank, followed the implosion of a system, based on non-existent collateral… A premature 'Credit Crunch' in fact!

And, all for a few cents worth of limo fuse wire… Oops!

Of course the cop let go of the power, unleashed the genie. He lowered his telescopic bike arms and the traffic flowed. The main artery surged with the life-force, pumping the City with its daily energy once more.

Meanwhile limo-life went on. We were stranded in a back-street of Queens, which was then considered a place one wouldn't venture into unless escorted by the cavalry… especially not in a stretched-limo. The car was hotting up because with no electrics the air conditioning was no longer working and this was steamy high summer. In fact the car was now cooking us. We were forced to use our initiative to keep cool. We didn't quite resort to singing songs to keep our spirits up, but we did make use of Coke cans from the limo's fridge. What the affluent have to suffer! We rubbed them over our sweating brows to keep ourselves from expiring.

Soon I thought, we would be safely transferred to another, working car. Then I saw the girls' faces freeze… and it wasn't the cold Coca Cola cans .

I was sitting with my back to the driver, the girls were facing me. Through the tinted window over my left shoulder, (I was told later) a man's hips had appeared; he stood almost against the car, reached down to his side and drew out a large revolver. Fiona went pale and genuinely couldn't speak...

So I asked , 'What's up, have they come to fix the car?' They both just nodded to what was going on over my shoulder.

I had a better view immediately, being able to see above his waistline... I was able to see the man's security-firm badge. It was just a cash-transfer from a supermarket into a bullet-proof van, with a couple of armed guards riding ' shot gun '. Obviously it was something they took seriously in Queens. The reaction was hardly surprising, because Pattie Hearst was D's cousin! Fear of kidnapping ran in the family.

The aeroplane to Ancona made a sudden bank to the right. I don't like it when pilots suddenly decide to ' fly ' the 'plane, as though they want to ' loop the loop ', out of the frustration of scheduled-flight boredom. It's gentler when they let the in-flight computer, do its thing. Apparently it's possible to let the computer fly you from A to B without any human intervention, even when landing it. I'm beginning to trust the '*Hal'* computer-driven World more than the human-driven one..... we're so susceptible to tummy bugs and drunken driving.

Below, I could see Venice. The Grand Canal glistened in the sun like a green Mamba, snaking its way through the terracotta roofs of the tiny island. We lurched again to the right to follow the Adriatic coast south. Once again we straightened out and my ears began to pop; a sure sign we'd started our descent. Probably only half an hour left, to reminisce...

I had been flicking through the brown envelopes at the Old Chapel, trying to glean a glimmer of pleasure amongst bills and circulars. I came across a white envelope with an embossed emblem of the Prince of Wales's three feathers. (We are both Welsh I must add, and the sight of those feathers started a small tingle that ran down my spine, past my bottom and even a bit down the back of the legs.... it might seem like I'm laying it on a bit thick but in that instant I was ready to fly the flag, take the colours, or even play full-back at rugby, if necessary).

I called Fiona, and we opened the letter together. I can't recall the exact words but it read something like this :

"His Royal Highness, The Prince Of Wales, would like to extend an invitation for you to have luncheon at Highgrove, and to come and see the Garden.

Yours sincerely,

Biggy Legge-Turke."

We are not staunch royalists, but we've always very much admired the Prince of Wales, because he fulfills his role in Britain with dignity and has had such a positive impact on environmental matters. He has been one of the main figures to encourage the growth of organic farming, and I think his questioning stance on architectural arrogance has also been a good thing. He's genuinely altruistic, and I think he is under-valued in our country for the enormous amount he's achieved.

I suppose we were invited to Highgrove because of our mutual interest in both painting and gardening.

But then we looked at the date on the invitation… ' Oh no! ' Fiona said,' I've got a feeling that's when we're on holiday in Italy, with Robin and Barbara.' ' I'll just go check in the diary …' and sure enough, we were going to be away.

So that was that, we couldn't go.

Oh well, we thought, it was nice to have been asked, but we felt we couldn't let our friends down, as we had already committed ourselves to the trip. When we told Robin about the invitation, he promised to wear his 'Spitting Image' Prince Charles mask to lunch that day, as compensation!

So we accepted that it had simply been a missed opportunity.

But then about a year later another of those envelopes arrived, a chance of a re-run and this time there was no way we were going to miss it...

So what to wear? The luncheon was in May, so maybe, I should finally invest in a linen suit - after all, it can be really hot in May sometimes, even in Gloucestershire. I hadn't owned a suit since school-days. I'd never had call for one, and had got away with borrowing one for the occasional wedding or funeral. I suppose if I was going to find an occasion for buying one this would be it.

As we drove towards Highgrove, it was evident from the cold wind and bending trees, that the choice of a pale linen suit was the wrong one. Never mind, I thought the excitement of the occasion will keep me warm. Also hundreds of people packed into a marquee is bound to create a bit of heat. (We could see a large marquee in the grounds of Highgrove and so assumed that's where we were heading.)

We parked in an empty car park some way from the house. It all seemed rather quiet and I looked at my watch... yes, dead on time,

"Have we got the right day ? " Fiona asked.

"Yes don't worry, it's definitely today- we've probably just taken a wrong turn and we'll come across another car park soon, full of people going to lunch,"

We eventually found ourselves in the house, but seemingly we'd entered through the wrong entrance. We pitched up right behind a valet who hadn't heard us, and was standing with his back to us, facing the front-door, a tray of drinks in hand.

I tapped gently... from behind, he appeared to levitate... I closed my eyes and waited for the sound of smashing glasses. But like a true pro, he landed, swayed the tray in a clock-wise circle until it balanced again.... without spilling a drop.

" Sorry ," I said, " we've been invited to lunch with the Prince of Wales... but we have no idea where to go?" I assumed the valet was waiting to meet the VIPs, and that we'd be shown into an ante-chamber from where we would be guided to the marquee.

" Just come in here and wait... please." He showed us into an adjacent room. Surely any minute now we'd be escorted to the marquee with all the other guests.... but then, coming along the corridor, we heard footsteps and the unmistakeable voice as He came through the door ....

" Ah... the Owens ," He said, adjusting his cufflink under the sleeve of his blazer , " You were supposed to come here last year, weren't you? It's such a shame you couldn't make it. That was a really hot day". (I'm sure He had spotted my light-weight suit by now). Some famous comedians had been there, and they'd all worn silly hats in the garden, not the same this year for us unfortunately, with the cold wind.

We were handed a gin and tonic as the other guests arrived (twelve in all, so no big tent for us, after all) and asked if we'd like to have a look around the gardens. A selection of coats were offered in the hall, and we all helped ourselves to one, Fiona ended up wearing a coat that had apparently belonged to the Aga Khan.

It was a real treat to see the garden at last, having heard and read so much about it. It was a prime example of a garden of our time, it bears the hallmarks of all the great garden designers and luminaries from the world of design, and who were influential when the garden was being created, particularly, Miriam Rotheschild and Sir Roy Strong.

The large terrace had a formal structure, but pleasingly naturalised planting, huge terracotta pots stopped the vistas at the end of intersecting paths and despite the cold, it had an 'Italianate' feel. Plants were encouraged to spill over the edges in an unstructured and creative fashion. The cracks and joints in the paths which were made from Cotswold stone flags, were encouraged to sprout with small flowering plants like Thyme and Saxifrage.The overall effect was of a personal, restorative space - a place that felt as though the owner was not afraid to let Nature build up a head of steam and ' do its own thing '. It was interesting hearing about all the new environmentally-friendly ideas for the garden, like hay bales used to purify the water in the pond and the filtering of water through reed beds. We came across some brightly painted garden benches (the first time we'd seen it done in Britain at that time.) "The seats were inspired by Yves St Laurent's colourful garden in Marrakech - do you like them? I think their quite fun! " The Prince said, as he bent down to chuck a stick for one of the dogs.

Seeing the garden had an immediate influence on ours, because when we got home, we painted our garden furniture a variety of blues and violets which seemed daringly different from the conventional, white painted fashion of the time.

After lunch, He took us to his new venture, next to the house and just about to open: a little ' Highgrove ' shop for people visiting the garden on the various tours, somewhere to buy souvenirs. Manning the till Himself, , we must have been amongst the first customers too - The Prince of Wales sold us a little garden light (complete with the three feathers.)

Maybe we could hang it from a pergola or an olive tree in a new garden?

Now we were landing in the promisingly named *Raffaello Sanzio*' airport at Ancona - (amazing to have an airport named after the painter Raphael, we thought). To the left we could see the Conero Peninsula and Ancona bleached at sea level with a collar of mist... we lurched rather haphazardly on landing and the Italians onboard cheered and applauded, (something we discovered happens every time) - relieved to be back on the ground and also to be back in their homeland.

For us it was a kind of earthing too: What was the chance that the house, not even shown properly on the internet, would be worth this crazy dash half-way across Europe? It would probably be next to a motorway, or overlooking a factory. Perhaps because of its price, disappointment was almost inevitable.....

SNOWING AND GROWING

The virtual house-hunting game had turned into reality. Only a week earlier we'd had no idea we would be in Italy, looking for our little 'retreat'.

We hired a small Italian car at the airport and headed up the coast. At Senigallia the Adriatic looked decidedly ' pearly ' in the opalescent light. It was early spring, but we'd never experienced Le Marche in March before; it was shockingly cold. Silly when I think back, but the word 'chilly' and Italy being in the same sentence hadn't occurred to me. It was however still beautiful, just very different from my mental picture of Italy, an image built from years of mid-summer, holiday heat and the constant quest for shade.

This light was hazy and the buildings appeared to be blue with cold. Trellises were naked of leaves and the streaks of copper sulphate from vine-spraying now showed up on the cracked stucco like varicose veins. Bare pergolas looked skeletal next to the walls of the houses and cast delicate shadows across the pastel shades of the buildings. Tiles on the roofs were held down belt and bracers fashion by large boulders, to protect the roofs from severe weather. Although made of terracotta, the tiles were no longer an earthy warm colour, but bleached white with a rime of frost... they looked more like curved slabs of interlocking ice.

Smoke twisted around the landscape, wrapping it in fine veils like tissue paper, resembling a Christo sculpture. The smoke came from fire-places and stoves greedily consuming the neat stacks of wood beside every house. All the wood-piles had been organised with pride, long before the end of summer, and were stacked in regimented and graded sizes. It was the only outward sign to the neighbours that life inside the house was carrying on with efficiency and normality through the winter months.

Each dip, valley and fox hole was filled with translucent mist, now turning milky in the siesta-time sunlight. This was a very different Italy for us, nothing like the summer place we knew. Where were the plastic chairs outside every front door...(even on busy streets) ? Where, too, were the terraces overflowing with bright pelargoniums and the circles of shade under colourful umbrellas? Gone were the sleeping dogs in the middle of the baking roads, gone were the cats seeking out tigered shadows... and gone were the people... where were the people ? That's what was so noticeably different; we had only ever seen Italy busy with people. People living life outside in the summer months....

Now there were no nut-brown elders chatting under nut-trees or playing cards outside bars; no tattooed teenagers walking arm in arm with their *nonna*, or business-men shouting loudly on their mobiles. No helmetless kids buzzing on mopeds or relaying their echoed brags up alleyways... this was a human-less, and almost soundless landscape, apart from the occasional gripe of a distant chain-saw. The contrast between the seasons was far more noticeable than in Britain.

We found a simple map of the whole Marche region, in the hire-car. It barely showed the main roads, and minor roads had been brushed aside as if the cartographer had been in a rush to meet someone for an *espresso*.

We decided that although our appointment with the estate agent was the following morning, we would try to find the house beforehand. To help us, we had not only the map but also the computer print-out and tantalising photo of the view. The estate agent had agreed that the next day we would meet in Arcevia. He had said that we would have to follow him to the house because apparently it was difficult to find.

Heading inland to Arcevia, we didn't hold out much hope of finding the actual property but thought it would be interesting to see the surrounding area anyway. We stopped on the flattish land leading to the hill-town; it was time at last to gather our thoughts - the day so far had been all rush, rush. Up at four o'clock to drive to Stansted from Gloucestershire with the hope of avoiding hold-ups on the M25, then the flight and lastly the car hire… all done in a frenzy of anticipation.

There was a real need to make physical contact with this unfamiliar, wintery Italy. So we got out of the car and leant on its cold wing for a few moments to gather our thoughts and take in the frosty unfamiliarity.

"Well, this it," I said. I think I was in some sort of delayed shock. The cold slapped my face, helping me to feel the sobering reality of where we were.

"I know… and isn't it wonderful," Fiona replied, not the slightest doubt in her voice.

We breathed in the freezing air that was tinged with woodsmoke and impending snow. Across the road, the fields stretched out in wide stripes of furrowed earth. To one side, tortured vines wired to ranks of vine posts climbed a hill. Each plant seemed to be pleading for spring with black-fingers clawing upwards.

I held my hands in front of my eyes, my fingers and thumbs interlocking to make a temporary picture frame. What I captured was an image of abstract swirling linear patterns in subtle earthy tones. For a few moments I held that miniature ' Paul Nash ' landscape in my hands (I could almost feel the presence of Henry Tonks, Head of Drawing at the Slade School of Art, leaning over my shoulder and asking the question; "what could be considered a perfect composition?" - and I could have answered "this might well be it.").

Stark trees remained standing in the middle of ploughed fields. Each tree had earned a soloist's respect from the farmer, and had been ploughed around, in harmony with the lines of a score. There was a harsh gash of white in the distance - a *strada bianca*, resembling a healing scar on the surface of the land, winding its way to a solitary farm. Cypress trees, diminished in 'Golden' perspective, and lined the road like pins on a map, reminding us where we were.

Ahead in the distance we could see the impressive sight of Arcevia, perched on the top of a hill that faded in colour, downwards from the summit, as if it was being drained of its life force by the cold. It seems to me that Arcevia has been overlooked as a sightseeing place (thankfully) - maybe it hasn't been spotted because it sits so high above eye-level...

The *Duomo* and various towers punctured the horizon and were visible from several miles away, but strangely, one loses sight of the town for a short while, when about a mile away, as the road twists through vineyards, it disappears amongst the undergrowth. Then suddenly it's towering above you again like a thought.

Two thousand feet of hill covered with two thousand years of habitation. Buildings climbing the slope out of control, coated in pasta-coloured plaster; houses, churches and factories clinging to the incline like newly kneaded, tacky dough, each structure trying to make an architectural statement. Slowly, as we watched, the hill was being eaten by a masticating Marche mist. Snow was also waving over and obscuring its edges.

"Let's park half way up and walk through the snowy lanes to the top," said Fiona. We climbed in the car as far as we could, but soon the snowdrifts at the sides of the road started to meet in the middle and we were forced to stop.

As we left the little Fiat, we left the twenty-first century too. It was time-travel, on foot. We were taken back to an era of narrow alleys where strange odours wafted from gutters and drains. Snow was finding its way between the roofs of the tall buildings and landing in slippery humps on the cobbles. It had white-lined all the balcony rails and wrought iron twirls and even the sides of empty pots were scribbled over with crude white marks like a child's chalk drawing of frost.

The snow on the criss-cross of wires overhead occasionally slipped off in front of us, making perfect stripes across the path. Its slow sloughing filled the air… we stopped for a breather: The only sound was of snow wheezing as it heaved off the over-filled edges and ledges. We climbed on upwards through alleyways and deserted narrow streets. The light was beginning to fade and it was only mid-afternoon. The large flakes screwed and scoured the air between the buildings and then were sucked back up in draughts.

This snow had given up the law of gravity for a life of lawless confusion, it was coming at us from all directions. Flecks of snow, in clouds like Saturniidae, seemed to be attracted to the orange street-lights, giving them halos of gold like frescoes.

Suddenley we emerged from an alleyway into the open, and found ourselves in the snowy main piazza - Piazza Garibaldi. To our amazement because of the complete quiet, it was full of people - silent people. It must have been most of the town's populace. They were standing around in sad-looking groups with solemn faces, all were dressed in heavy black coats. A funeral was taking place, and evidently it was a funeral for someone of local importance. As we started to cross the ancient *piazza*, the peace was shockingly broken by a single bell from the *Duomo*, a heavy-metal sound resonated through stone and snow, and wavered in its intensity with the wind, finding corners to hide in. The mostly white-haired folk sloshed through the slush in time with to the death-knell, they seemed beckoned by the bell. The whole scene could have been from a black and white Fellini film; even two Benedictine nuns were there dressed in their stark, medieval-looking habits and strategically placed, like extras.

But this was very real. We felt like onlookers from a different planet, not fellow European citizens. We'd been eating a ' full-English ' only hours before. Now we were witnessing a moving and timeless Italian scene. The speed of travel trivialises reality.

The light was fading fast, as we drove down the slippery bends from the other side of Arcevia. We headed towards the peak-shrouded Appenines. The scenery on this side of the town was dramatically different; hills and vales spread out around the road as though unfurling towards the mountains, woodland areas stood out as purple bruises on the milky-white bosomy hills. The vineyards of the gentle slopes nearer the coast had gone. There were no more cypress trees or olive groves. This was a landscape I recognised from my childhood: the Welsh Marches, the land running along the border of Wales - could it be more than coincidence that the two landscapes bear the same name and look gegraphically similar? I certainly felt we were following some kind of primeval calling in the blood, returning to our Celtic roots, (especially as this was the main region of Italy that Celts had actually settled). The landscape certainly felt familiar.

Ribbons of pink mist were pulled like Bardic banners between the woodland peaks. Blurred edges of snow surrounded the fields in a Turner-esque manner, boundaries over-lapped each other in translucent layers, as when water-colours are used 'wet-on-dry'. It was still a man-managed landscape and yet awe-inspiring. It seemed tamed but also dramatic; a landscape that could satisfy all visual, spiritual and physical needs.

Reaching the base of a valley, we came across a road sign; "look" said Fiona,"San Giovanni - that's the address on this bit of the info., it must be up here... ". We turned left, followed the winding road and topped the hill near Castello... We started to recognise the lie of the land from the much studied computer print out.

" I reckon the photo was taken from about here but in the summer. Yes, look, there's the line of electricity poles - and those three oaks in a row... the house must be over there in amongst those trees," I said, stopping. I wound down the window, filling the car with icy air.

We drove through the small hamlet of San Giovanni, passing its pretty white church and stopped about fifty yards beyond the last house, on the very edge of the village. There was a snowy, overgrown track leading out of sight to the right. It went down into a wooded spur that seemed to launch itself into the vast view.

" Well, what do you think? This must be it. It's probably down that lane - do you fancy coming for a look?" I said.

Fiona looked dubiously down the disappearing woodland track, she seemed to have lost her nerve and said, " Tell you what; why don't you just pop your head around the corner - just in case there are vicious dogs or anything."

So off I went, the light was still just good enough to find footholds in the thick snow. Each footprint had stamped a blue comma as I looked back towards the car, Fiona... and warmth.

Was I going to find our future around that corner ?

My very first impression of the house was good. The elevation that faced me looked as though the place was actually being lived in. It appeared to be painted a grubby white. There was a small terrace with metal railings around it. A pan-tiled roof with boulders (to hold down the tiles) sticking out of the snow on a lean-to extension. A huge satellite dish, like something from a space station, with a tangled tagliatelle of snow-laden wires coming from it, was bolted to the eaves of the roof. Although not something we'd need, it made the building look lived in. Also, it meant there was electricity. I could see there was water too, because of an outside tap. So all the essentials were here.

This old farm-house looked like a place that was possible to revive. It was very much like our first cottage in Nailsworth - Ugly - rendered in grey cement with dark areas of staining caused by damp. The brown, louvered shutters were a bit shabby, too. But, it was a building more in need of loving care than a major renovation job. All the time, as I walked around the house, my eyes kept flitting towards the view. What a view. It was even better than the picture on the net. It wrapped around the house, and as I walked around the boundary the view was glimpsed between the trees - a flickering animation.

Deep snow covered the flat area around the house (there were clumps of snow covering mounds of long grass - it was certainly too uneven to call it a lawn) and a stark lattice-work of trees formed a screen around the edge of the property. There were oaks, an almond, a walnut, acacias, a Judas tree, interspersed with fig trees, all distinctive even without their summer plumage. Beyond the line of trees, the land dropped steeply away into a valley. Then, valley after valley, hundreds of fields unfolded each one a different shape from generations of changing and inherited boundaries.

Some fields were already ploughed, primed for spring, but at that moment looked pin-striped with snow. A few were dotted with newly-planted rows of trees. I could even make out occasional olive groves and vineyards on the south-facing slopes, which was a surprise at this altitude. Warm, occupied houses where the snow had melted off their roofs, glowed orange. They stood out against the snow, their cosy lights pricking the dimness like a star-chart.

The view spread out in front of me, hill beyond hill, like breathing waves on a landlocked sea, rhythmically rising and falling. Each dip was drowned by a misty spume and each swell was topped with a surf of snow... cast-away on the surface was the flotsam of farms and jetsam of houses, fading into the smudged horizon to the very edge of the known World.

The panorama was vast.

Every degree of the compass, from West to East contained a complete view - just one degree would be satisfying, but in front of me there was a span of two hundred and fifty or more degrees. As a full-stop to the right, ancient Arcevia was perched on the top of a hill, almost quivering in the cold air above its prey - as if it was a hawk about to swoop down the valleys from a knight's gauntlet. It was indeed a timeless land, with its Renaissance painting hills covered in forests for hunting and apart from the boundaries of fields, largely unchanged since Signorelli had lived here, over five hundred years before. For me, it is a landscape easier to describe in paint than in words, but whatever the medium, it would be impossible to convey the magnificence of the scenery without resorting to silly exaggeration... so here goes;

I can only say that to fully appreciate the many-layered depths of such a view - artistically, poetically, idealistically and hedonistically, it helps to appreciate the concept of 'Arcadia,' created in the eighteenth century by garden designers and painters or alternatively, share the visions of a new world experienced by Humphry Davy after a whiff of nitrous oxide, or the laudanum-induced 'Wonderland-scapes' of the nineteenth century, the fantasy of Tolkien's Mordor and the Shire, and of course the twentieth century insight beyond all others that was induced by LSD which created a psychedelic mindscape...

or, simply, to believe that there could be a 'Promised Land'.

But back to the chilled here and now, with the clichéd climax of an apocalyptic movie - on a wooded hill in the near distance, a metal cross caught the last ray of sunlight.

In the garden, a leafless fig tree spread its branches over a solid shed - it looked functionally rustic, with its dove-cote and terra-cotta roof. Leaning on the back wall, higgledy-piggledy, was a pile of old wire-fronted cages for rabbits. The snow had now found shelter in the cages, etching white each hexagon of chicken-wire. They looked like hives for giant, albino bees.

The snow was over knee-deep and every step sighed as the surface was punctured. Where it had drifted, in the lowest part of the garden, bleached stalks of umbellifae stuck out shambolically, and their ghosting shadows, still just visible, twitched in the breeze.

A dog's chain was tied around a concrete post, staining it with red/brown, sanguineous streaks. At the end of the garden, another concrete structure - probably a kennel - was snow-filled and teetering over the edge of the land, on the verge of escape.

As I looked back at the house from the edge of the land, I had a strong feeling that it was waiting for someone to come and nurture it. It certainly needed to be rescued from the cold.

I retraced my foot prints back up the track, my socks and trouser legs were taut with ice. Fiona was still waiting patiently in the steamed-up car.

"Well?" She asked pleadingly, as though I'd taken a bit too long.

It was very tempting to tease, (I have learnt, however, that it's not always the right thing to do!). Anyway, I really didn't have the heart to spoil such an important moment.

" It was amazing," I said, " far better than I expected. It really doesn't look too bad at all ... a lot like our first cottage; a touch of render here and there, and a spot of paint, and it'll be fine. Come on, there aren't any dogs, let's both go down and have a look."

So off we trudged, wet shoes getting even wetter. We retraced my snow-prints around the outside of the house and agreed that if it was only half as good on the inside , then, it really could be possible.

We were in a state of euphoria when we returned to the car. We stood next to it, looking west, towards the high Apennines. The sun had set now but there was still a last light-show of apricot rays shooting out from behind the peaks.

" I can't believe that those mountains could, if we're lucky... be part of our life," Fiona sighed: " I always wanted to be Heidi."

We spent the night at Peter and Richard' s house. They had a rule that any friends buying a house in Italy had to be outside their ten kilometre exclusion-zone. I don't really think they would have enforced this rule!

We were in the clear anyway, because ' ours ' really was far enough away. But I could see their point so we made a pledge to ourselves that we wouldn't ever bother them over any troubles that may lie ahead.

Surprisingly, the 'boys' didn't know Arcevia well and had only passed through it a couple of times when researching for their regional guide-book. We were sitting around the kitchen table chatting and eating supper, when Richard casually dropped a bit of a bombshell;

" You say the house is near Montefortino?" He paused then leant across and asked Peter, " Isn't that where all those protests were a few weeks ago - you know, about that quarry being extended? " Peter shook his head, he looked slightly embarrassed, " I don't know - yes, maybe? "

" You are joking ? " I said. I really hoped they were just winding us up; " ... aren't you?"

They both looked at me with horrible solemnity.

" Oh well, that's it then," I said, absolutely devastated. I paused over my pasta , " that explains why it's so cheap... I knew there had to be a snag."

"Are you sure the quarry's near the house?" asked Fiona: "because if we can't hear it, or see it, I still want to go ahead... oh, I hope we haven't come all this way for nothing."

"Hold on, hold on," Richard said, donning his 'council-for-the-defence' face; " sorry - I haven't told you the whole story, because," he paused yet again, " I went to the *comune* offices in Arcevia on Friday, as you'd said in your email that the house you'd seen on the net was near Arcevia, I thought it best to check. I looked at the plans for the quarry - you can do that you know…"

He dithered, being deliberately 'Rumpolesque'.

"Yes, Richard, and …?"

"Well, seemingly, they're developing the other side of the mountain. There is going to be a new quarry, but nowhere near you. The old quarry - which is a couple of miles from you - is to be closed. So good news all round… cheers!" He downed a glass of Barolo, and we joined him, feeling slightly shaken but also relieved.

Not only had Richard bothered to go all that way to check out the plans, which in itself was hugely considerate, but he also said that he would be happy to come and see the house with us the following day, if we would like.

"That would be brilliant, Richard, because you know the area a bit, and, help with the translation would be good, as we're learning Italian and it's *molto lento,* " I said, raising my glass again.

We woke early for our meeting with the estate agent. Out of the window, a placid pink light stroked the edges of the pergola. It was sunny but looked cold - all the colours were bleached and it reminded me of an Eric Ravilious lithograph; frosty cross-hatching made a sgraffito of the worked earth which had the base colour of litho-stone. Steam was rising gently as the sun warmed the paving on the terrace, in front of me.

I felt nervous… Today really could be a life-changing day. The cold air and bright sunlight felt alpine fresh as we got in the car. Richard tilted the front-seat for Fiona to get in the back.

The arrangement was that we would meet outside the bar in Piazza Garibaldi in Arcevia, so we hoped the snow had been cleared a bit from the day before.

We had arranged to meet at ten-thirty. We arrived in time for a coffee at the bar, in the Piazza. By eleven o'clock we started to get anxious... where was he? There was no phone call from him... did I even have his number? We all scanned the property details; a small number was written in pencil - maybe I had jotted it down at home, although I had no memory of it. I rang it: ' Pronto' the English voice came loud and clear. ' Jeff here...'

" Oh hello, it's Signor Owen here, we're in Arcevia, where are you?"

"Yeah, sorry about that, " Jeff replied in an extremely casual manner, " been caught in a bit of an avalanche on the road. It often happens here this time of year - look, have a coffee or something, will be a bit late, bye!"

About an hour, and several coffees later, a small car arrived in the piazza. It drove around the mound of scraped-up snow in the centre, and parked outside the bar.

The car seemed overfilled with people. Flattened limbs made dark patches on the condensed windows. Only four people were in the car, but as they emerged we could see they were all quite large. Jeff was at least six foot five, and probably in his late twenties; the other man was almost the same height but far more bulky. The two women with them were also fairly tall. Quite an impressive amount of humanity to squeeze into a small Lancia, and really a lot more than the one estate agent we had been expecting.

Jeff strode towards us with giant steps, kicking up arctic rolls with his size fourteen shoes. His shaking-hand was poised: " Mr Owen, yeah, I'm sorry about being late... we weren't actually stuck in an avalanche, but we had to do a detour because of one, right around Sassoferrato - the road was closed."

Jeff turned, and waved forward his entourage " Anyway...this is Alessia, Maria and Bruno."

Bruno moved towards us with the rolling gait of a prop-forward and looked like Bluto, the bad guy of Popeye. He had Manet-black hair, bushy stubble and forbidding eyebrows. He could have been a pirate or a cartoon robber in his spare time. He certainly didn't look like the kind of estate agent you'd want to entrust your cash with.

Then Jeff introduced us and when Bruno smiled his whole character changed - he morphed into Bruno-the-cuddly-bear! I've never witnessed two extremes in a person's personality so quickly, before. (Watching Dr.Jekyll change springs to mind, but Mr.Hyde might have made a pretty convincing estate agent!)

Jeff introduced us to the others; " Alessia is my partner - we run the British website, and Bruno and Maria are the local estate agents. The house we are going to see is on their books; now where is it ? Oh yeah, San Giovanni. Follow us I guess..."

Like origami people they folded their bodies back into the car in reverse order from the way they'd emerged, like rewinding a film. We followed behind them in our car .

The three of us agreed as we followed, that apart from the rather awe-inspiring first sight of Jeff and Bruno they did seem approachable. The fact that we wouldn't have to go through the whole morning in our shaky Italian was also a relief.

We took the route that we had taken the day before and parked in the same place. I was hoping no-one would notice all the footprints heading down the track. We both felt guilty that we had already looked at the house from outside.

Jeff came towards me, looking down at the clipboard of papers in his hand; " Mr. Owen I've just noticed something here," his voice seemed troubled.

" Oh-no," I thought, he's angry that we've already been here, yesterday.

"I've just noticed something here. You're from Chalford, Gloucestershire?" he asked, reading from the clipboard like someone doing a street questionnaire.

"Yes that's right... why is that a problem?"

He paused, still looking at the clipboard.

It was as though what was in front of him was causing him the problem. He could not digest the facts. He looked up at last and both his eyebrows rose in incredulity.

" No, no... it's just that I'm from Eastcombe, and I'm sure I've been to an exhibition at your Old Chapel!"

As far as I was concerned, Jeff had come from Ancona, so I too was amazed. Eastcombe is the next village to Chalford. With a coincidence like that, we felt the outcome of the day must be guided by fate.

Coincidence or fate - is it significant? Whether one thinks of it as important or not these things happen to all of us. Aren't we all supposed to be linked to everyone else on the planet by a common friend or something in a chain of no more than six people? One can usually find some kind of link with a complete stranger.

For instance; our son Laurie lives with a girl as a housemate in London. He didn't know her before college or from Gloucestershire, but it just so happens, coincidentally, that her family live in the house that I lived in as a child.

She actually grew up in the same bedroom as me, we were nurtured in the same nest, watched the sun and moon journey across the same walls through our separate childhoods but there are forty years between our mutual occupation of that small space on Earth. and now she lives with my son. Think of all the houses in London and multiply them by all houses in Gloucestershire, not to even mention all the bedrooms just in our small country. What are the chances? But the most extraordinary thing to me is that no one else

I tell seems to find it the slightest bit odd or intriguing.

Now is that just a chance thing or should we find a deeper meaning in these paths that cross like ley lines in all our lives? There is a theory that we live many lives every time with the same characters, who in each life take a different role. So maybe in a past life I was Jeff's hamster, or perhaps he was my dog or my wife…

Who knows?

One of the best coincidence stories I ever heard, was told by Barney, a teacher at the school our children went to. Barney was a great outward-bound kind of bloke. We felt very happy to entrust our kid's safety with him on the many camps and adventures that the school did. He even took them right across Europe in an old van... a fantastic two-month long cultural ' Grand Tour '. He's the most placid, ex-Para you could ever wish to meet.

On one of his sabbaticals he was touring Australia on foot with the most basic of survival equipment. On his way from Alice Springs to Darwin, in the baking outback, he said that things were getting slightly worrying: he was running out of water and it doesn't take very long for the situation to become dangerous under that punishing sun. The only option was to get to the nearest highway as quick-ly as possible; he needed to flag down a vehicle - probably one of those massive road-trains, not easily done because they take about a mile to stop.

He told the story brilliantly in an end of term assembly; he built the drama … from the first sighting of a dust-cloud in the distance, then spotting the speck on the horizon; a truck. He stood in the road, waved and willed it to stop. Fortunately it saw him in time to pull up.

Climbing up into the air-conditioned cab he was welcomed by the driver: a big, hairy Aussie.

" Alright mate, where you going? Darwin - O.K. jump in then,"

Barney was hugely relieved to be out of the intense heat and they soon got chatting;

" So mate, where are you from?" the Aussie asked.

Barney relaxed in the cool cab, and replied,

" I'm from the UK ."

" Oh yeah, I know Britain mate - where in Britain ?"

"Well, Gloucestershire."

"Yeah, I know Gloucestershire mate, whereabouts?"

"A small town called Stroud , you won't have heard of it I don't supp…"

" Oh yeah, I know Stroud… whereabouts in Stroud?"

" Well not actually in Stroud, I come from a little village outside Stroud called Chalford," Barney said in disbelief.

" Oh yeah… I know Chalford… whereabouts in Chalford, mate…?"

"This is ridiculous." Barney said, ' I live at the far end of the village a place called Valley Bottom but there are only about five houses there.'

The Aussie kept looking straight ahead at the road, and with no emotion in his voice said matter-of-factly: " Oh yeah, I know Valley Bottom mate, I used to live there.'

Now even if you don't believe in fate it is an amazing and true story. This hairy guardian angel had possibly saved Barney's life… and also knew all his neighbours.

The fact that Jeff came from the next village to us in Gloucestershire, must have had some effect on our feeling about the day. It was as though the ' Gods ' were with us, or the entrails were doing whatever entrails are supposed to do. We were 1,500ft up a hillside in a strange land and yet it already seemed so right. There was a familiarity about the place, and we hadn't even crossed the threshold yet.

The house had been split into two separate dwellings by two brothers who apparently didn't get on. Each part had two bedrooms, a kitchen, bathroom and sitting room.

A man from the village was introduced to us and we gathered his name was Edris, and he had the keys to let us in. He opened the ubiquitous golden metal and glass door which had no doubt been very trendy in the 70's. We felt the warmth of the place as the door opened, even though it had been empty for a couple of years. Now the house was being bathed in a strenthening spring sunshine, yesterday's cold was gone, the snow could only survive in the garden's shadiest corners.

The room we entered was a kitchen, it was practical and certainly compact. The initial impression was that it was well appointed in the rustico style. My first thought, was how woody it was. Orange coloured pine seemed to cover every surface including the ceiling. A pine table took up most of the kitchen-living area. There was a small fireplace at one end, a paraffin range along the far wall and a wooden dresser on the other. A diminutive sink was on the other wall placed at mid-thigh height. It felt like a log-cabin for *Munchkins*.

As with viewing any house (in my experience) that you're about to commit a great deal of effort and cash into, we probably only took a couple of seconds walking through the room, one would put more thought into buying a pair of pliers. We just kept thinking yes, that's OK... let's get on to the next bit... Climbing the sturdy marble staircase, we passed an incongruous girlie calendar on the wall (the sort you'd normally associate with a tyre-fitters garage), and then onwards to the first floor.

The first bedroom was cosy, decorated in 'Grandma' style circa 1930. There was an aroma of lavender talc and face powder, a little lace-edged cloth covered up the nakedness of the dressing table.The bedroom was quite spacious but with everyone in a line around the edge of the bed it felt as claustrophobic as a wake. They seemed to be all talking at the same time, very loudly, in Italian.

Then suddenly there was a lull.

Pointing at me, Alessia, asked abruptly; " what's that under your arm?"

" It' s a guide book of the Marche, why?"

" I thought it was." She said , "that's a fantastic book, where did you get it, I've been trying to get another copy for years ?"

" Well actually he gave it to me no sorry, he wrote it , maybe he'll give you a copy too!"

Richard modestly took the praise - Alessia said it was by far the best guide book of the Marche in English. Richard wasn't needed as much as we had expected for his interpreting, as Jeff spoke Italian and Alessia spoke English. However, with his legal astuteness he was aware of possible pitfalls and kept us updated on what was being said, deciphering the wall of sound. It was vital to have good hearing, as it was so noisy in the small rooms with eight people who all seemed to be shouting in Italian. I kept looking to see if Richard was as impressed with the place as we were. At that stage, with his continual firing of strategic questions, it was difficult to gauge what he was thinking.

Obviously we were already very taken with the place, but there was one particular moment that sold the house to us; up in the bedroom that I had already mentally marked as ours, Jeff, with a shove, opened first one shuttered window then the other. The sudden exposure to the landscape was heart stopping. What he revealed was a view above the tree height that we hadn't seen before. It felt like the scene in the film ' A Room with a View' when the *Duomo* in Florence is seen through a *pensione* window for the first time.

I imagined throwing open those shutters every morning.

I kept reliving that moment mentally, even just after it had happened. I could visualise them just before they were opened. There was an unexplainable calmness about the position of the windows which were set at right angles in Le Marche architectural style, one on each wall; it was like actually standing in a muted interior painted by Vilhelm Hammershøi, where one grey tone is laid upon another in subtle layers. But when opened, thrillingly, the outside light flooded the corner of the bedroom. The drama of the transition from shuttered darkness into bright sunlight was equivalent to emerging from an afternoon in the Frasassi caves.

Opening those windows changed the question of whether we *should* buy the place to *where do we sign*? With a twist of handle and rattle of glass, the old windows opened again and again in my mind and in poured the light, air, spring warmth and birdsong - in poured Italy.

The journey here, from computer print-out, the M25 at dawn and trailing across Europe in the snow - now it all made sense. This was the place that had been lurking in the back of my consciousness for decades, and the windows being opened had symbolically released it's spirit. It felt as if a force had pulled us towards the house, much as William's tumbling pigeons had been drawn to the ground. There was no question of looking at any other properties in the area.

We still had the rest of the house to see. Now, with minds made up, even the tiny bathroom looked passable. (It did however have strange black-marbled tiles on the floor, each tile had a pattern that looked exactly like ladies bits! What kind of person had lived here?)

By the time we entered the *cantina* (an area beneath the house, where, we were told that animals had once been kept to provide 'under-floor' heating), I felt like I was selling the property to Jeff rather than the other way round.

" Look at these concrete beams," I pointed out. " They look good, this work must have been done quite recently. It's really not in too bad a state..." I said as a huge chunk of render came away just by brushing past it.

There was no key to the other part of the house, but Edris the sprightly old man, pulled a bit of string hanging over the shutter and it opened. With the agility of a twenty-year-old he hoisted himself through the window and opened the door from the inside.

The plaster board ceiling was hanging off the joists and covered in black mould. There were hideous kitchen cupboards on the sitting-room walls and other alterations we would have to make, little DIY jobs too boring to mention. Nothing could put us off by now. Apart from these minor faults the place seemed reasonably sound. We figured that even the 'avocado' bathroom suite would soon be back in vogue!

Wandering back outside we couldn't see any major problem. All of us walked to the edge of the garden. Standing in some snow left in a shaded spot next to the old kennel, Alessia pointed down to the garden boundary and wooded valley; " All this comes with the house" she said, pointing vaguely.

"What, do you mean down to that row of oak trees?" I thought she meant the boundary was the first row of trees, some ten metres away. That would be plenty to cope with, I thought.

"No... no, see beyond, in the valley, I think it's about seven of your English acres, and there's an allotment in the village, isn't that right Jeff?"

" Yeah, I think so, 'course we'll have to get all the boundaries sorted, an' that", Jeff said.

"Almost enough space for your little Italian country garden then Fi, eh?" I said sarcastically, (whilst also thinking of all the work). I scanned the densely wooded valley, darned or quilted with cotton strands of snow.

We were in shock, the whole thing seemed too good to be true.

Was there a catch ? If we say yes, does it simply become ours?

I could feel heat from the spring sun radiating off a wall of the house as we walked past it ... Fiona was beaming too. We had a very quick nod and a wink at each other. I took it to mean we were positive . I looked up at Jeff and said ,' Well I think we want to buy it , so what happens now? '

" Great, well Freddie (we were already on first name terms), all I've got to do is go back to the office and make a few calls . I should be able to let you know within a couple of days - I can't see that there's going to be a problem.."

We walked up the track back to the cars. I was feeling wobbly with the adrenalin, and the caffeine from earlier. I had a ringing sound between my ears.

Even Richard, cautiously, seemed to think it was a good deal.

Saying you agree to buy a place in Italy is not the end of the matter. Even if you're able to stump up the vendor's asking price without a quibble or a haggle, it doesn't just become yours.

However, in our heads it was a time for celebration. We dropped Richard back at his home. We decided to fill the rest of the day with a road-trip to explore the area, and climbed by car to the top of Frontone with its fortress that for several years we'd watched, lit up on summer nights, from the boys' house. The sun had disappeared once more sending the temperature very quickly back to zero. Everything was icy again but the sight of Le Marche spreading out from Frontone's ramparts, as white as Fabriano water-colour paper, and the feeling of excitement, warmed us inside, like a pilot light, soon this place may be part of our world too. It made me remember the tour of Le Marche we'd had with Richard years before, and reminded me how different the temperature could be.

We kept driving - marvelling at the beauty of the area. It was a way of mentally staking a claim to it, just like any other animal marking its territory. We walked through the old magnificent centre of Fabriano and looked for somewhere to have a late lunch, to celebrate our new home in Italy, we couldn't find a single restaurant, pizzeria or snack bar. It was the off season for eating-out. Our spirits could not be broken, and in the end we sat on a park bench in the cold, and nibbled on a piadina. There, in front of us, was a rendered house that had been painted what would be the perfect colour for ' our ' house: it was a bright, pinky/orange colour that seem to throw the light back even in the afternoon's gloom, and its turquoise shutters were exactly the same tone. The combination zinged.

" Can you imagine, *if* we *do* get the house? We could paint it that colour, and it would lift our spirits even on the dullest day."

" Yes, and it would be great, because you'd be able to see the house from the moon too! " Fiona giggled ... (it's not her place to make the jokes!)

The process of buying a house in Italy, involves commitment immediately. The very next day, we had to meet Jeff and Alessia in Ancona to get a *codice fiscale*, or personalised code, even though we had no idea if our offer on the house was going to be accepted. The number is needed for everything, like opening a bank account, hospital visits, leasing a gas cylinder or even becoming a *family friend* at Ikea .

Jeff and Alessia were really helpful guiding us through those initial legal steps. They took us to the appropriate office in Ancona, and made sure we signed in all the right places. Jeff was, as always, his cool, unflustered self. As we said goodbye we felt like they were old friends.

" Yeah Freddie just don't worry about it it'll be fine, I'll be in touch in a couple of days with the good news, bye.... yeah bye."

Our whirlwind trip was over and on the flight back we tried to take stock of our thoughts. There was certainly no need to look back through our memories like on the way out to Italy - we were planning for a new future.

Good as his word within a few days Jeff phoned....

"Oh, Hi Freddie, Jeff here, well not such good news actually, they now want a hundred thousand euro."

I was genuinely shocked, it was a ridiculous leap in price, a third as much again. I think I blurted out a couple of rude words, it was a sort of reflex, but luckily it had the desired response from Jeff.

"Alright, then Freddie - I think you've made your side clear... I'll tell them what you said, ... well, not exactly!" He chuckled, and put the phone down.

Not that he was trying it on, nor indeed was I. In Italy, the system of house buying, we found out later, works differently from ours. If someone shows an interest in your property... you ask for more money.

There was a ping-pong game of phone calls. Although the one apartment was being sold by the daughter of Luigi Tristallini, the other belonged jointly to five daughters of his deceased brother. They lived all over Europe so each one had to be contacted, every time there was a new offer. A very longwinded process for Jeff and Alessia.

Eventually, a satisfactory price for all parties was reached, but it took several weeks. The price rose a bit but not too drastically, and some of the furniture was to be thrown in. Then we were told that in Italy, the price of the agreed sale had to be published in the locality for three months, if the property was rural, to make sure that no farmers with bordering land wanted it as they have first refusal on the land. I think that the property had been on the market for a couple of years already, so it seemed unlikely that somebody might want it, but one never knows.

Modern Italians seem very reticent about buying old rural places. It appears that they would rather move into a modern concrete block of flats than be tarnished by the *contadino* label. The stigma of being a rural peasant lies deep in the psyche; it is only a generation or so ago that the rural classes lived under a system of tied serfdom. Much of the land was owned by the church, or landlords, and both kept the peasant farmers trapped in a regime of debt and near starvation. Maybe that's why the nostalgic wave for back to the country rural life hasn't been as popular in Italy, as in Britain.

Trying to analyse why someone of my generation is drawn towards older buildings is really quite a difficult question to answer. Modern buildings are logically much easier to live in, I know that - no leaking roofs, no toxic lead pipes, no cracks or draughts and no weekends wasted trying to find the source of a strange odour.

But perhaps saving time isn't everything; maybe it's healthy for the brain to be occupied by a constant stream of trivial problems created by an older property, otherwise it finds the space for other neuroses... or even proper work.

I know that for me it is a kind of therapy solving the small problems. I get a tiny dose of satisfaction each time I manage to bodge a thing, even when I know full well it should have been taken on by a real expert.

As to why I am so drawn to old buildings, maybe it's the natural reaction against where I had been brought up. I grew up in a modern house. So what made me rebel, aesthetically? I have my parents to thank for my love of antiquity: they were responsible for sending me to an old school, not a posh school, just a very old one. Just recently I looked up The King's School, Gloucester where I was educated, on the internet. It said that it was apparently one of the oldest documented schools in the World. I already knew it was pretty old, because we had always been told that Henry VIII had granted its charter as a school. Also as boys we knew that William the Conquerer commissioned the Domesday Book in the room where we did all our exams. What I hadn't realised until very recently was that it had been a school for over eight hundred years, at first for monks; when reading Geraldis Cambrensis' (Gerald of Wales) " Tour of Wales," I discovered that he had attended my school in the 1140s. Perhaps this must be a contributory factor to why I'm comfortable and feel at home with old, well-worn things and have always sought out older places to live in. (They also filmed some of the Harry Potter books there, so I almost feel I went to Hogwarts!)

When at school, I was fascinated by all aspects of the incredible human achievement of that edifice; A massive Cathedral, built on boggy ground, that was still standing and as good as new eight centuries later. There was so much to be amazed at daily as I sat through the morning services; the Norman stone pillars and the huge flying buttresses, the recently-discovered painted organ pipes, and the enormous east window, which was the largest window in the world when it was made. I absorbed the whole experience of being in such an historic space every day, and felt that I belonged to that past a little, and it to me. Every day we walked under the webbed fan vaulting of the cloisters, passing the place where the monks had played 'Nine Men's Morris' or 'Fox and Geese' on rough lines carved into the stone, or washed in their cold stone sinks, eight centuries before. Most mornings we walked around the tomb of a king (Edward the Second). We schoolboys were fascinated by the king's demise; he came to a ' sticky end ,' so to speak, at Berkeley Castle, murdered by having a red hot poker rammed up his bottom.

If, on some odd occasion, I was left alone in that vast building after a school concert, or exhibition in the Chapter House, the chilling weight of time felt like a tightening belt around the brain, like a contact with the spirits of the past . However, I still seek that elusive security that comes with something that has been around for a bit, and tood the test of time. There is something about the heaviness of an eight hundred-year-old oak door closing, that can't be replaced by MDF... and that smell of woodworm treatment that impregnates not only your clothing forever, but your very soul, so that no dwelling seems like home without it.

Living in a chapel is a small scale way of recapturing my youth. It is probably as close as one can get to living in a cathedral. There are reminders everywhere, such as the great doors with fancy iron hinges. It has a ludicrously big front door key. There is exquisite craftsmanship in the stone work and pitched-pine arched beams. It even has simple stained glass and carved stone mullion windows. It connects me to my happy childhood.

Thinking of stained glass reminds me of something; Fi's strange meeting with a fortune teller. When I very first met Fiona, we were both students and I was living in a caravan in the garden of her rented flat.

One day she asked me where I was born - she thought I came from Cheltenham, so when I said 'Brecon', her face went pale and she looked quite faint and ill.

I learned later that the day before, she had been to see a well respected gypsy fortune-teller down on Cardiff docks. The Romany lady had told Fiona that she was going to meet someone who had been born in Brecon. He was dark haired (me... then), and his father did something to do with design on large sheets of paper (architect). She foresaw that we would wrap up large parcels to send overseas (exhibitions abroad)... and most importantly, that we would live in a place with stained glass! We actually tried to make her prediction come true, by putting lots of stained glass in our first tiny cottage, but that could be seen as forcing the issue. The most obvious place to have stained glass is of course a church or chapel.

Another strange quirk of synchronicity or fate happened when we had outgrown our cottage in Nailsworth; Laurie had come along and suddenly we only had one bedroom between the three of us. The cottage just became too small. Now we needed a family-sized home. A small-holding of some sort would, we thought, be ideal for a more self-sufficient lifestyle. So we looked in *Dalton's Weekly*. Soon we came across just the thing in Pembrokeshire, near the coast. We travelled the four hours to get there, and the property looked good as we drove up to it; we could see it had buildings for studio space, a couple of acres of market garden and even a distant view of the sea. Perfect.

We knocked and an old man opened the door, he looked like a little Welsh wizard. The first thing he asked was where we had come from? said "Nailsworth" and it emerged that he knew our area better than we did!

Then he spake forth, like a mini-soothsayer:

" Where you want to move to, is Chalford... it's lovely there!"

"Hang on... What? But, don't you want us to buy this house?"

Within days, having never heard of Chalford before.

We found the chapel, and have lived here ever since.

Things went very quiet on the Italian front, for several months. We only had occasional phone calls from Jeff or Alessia. They were working very hard on our behalf trying to organise all the vendors, and also getting the land boundaries verified and legally registered. Jeff admitted to us later, that if it hadn't been for our tenuous link (Eastcombe / Chalford), he would have dropped the sale, simply because of the amount of paper-work. The property's boundaries should have been fixed before it was placed on the market. We knew that if we lost the house we would find nothing else as suitable. It was now touch and go.

Our dear friend, Valerie du Monceau (a feng shui consultant) suggested we make a scroll of the house details, wrap it in a red ribbon and put it in a south-facing window! We were willing to do anything at this stage so duly obeyed. Positive thoughts, we reckoned, might produce the vibes we needed.

Actually a similar thing had worked for Val - she had only just been through the whole process of buying a place in Italy herself; In a moment of clear thought, after trying to evaluate what she wanted out of life, she realised what she really wanted was a place in Venice. You may well be thinking as we did, at the time... 'we'd all like a place in Venice, Val... but get real!' I think the general consensus was that she was a bit crackers, after all Val is certainly not wealthy. She really focused positively, even putting a strange walking-stick thing with a crystal on top in her 'wealth corner'.

But blow me, she did it... She bought an apartment in the heart of Venice, with an ingenious juggling of finances. She now owns a tiny piece of that wonderful city.

It was June and we were walking around Truro Cathedral, waiting for Laurie's graduation ceremony, when the mobile phone rang... very loudly. I made for the door; it was Jeff, with the news that at last the house was ours.

We thought: " great, we can just pay the money and move straight in."

"Well Freddie , it's not like that in Italy," Jeff said , " No... see, what happens now is you'll come over to pay a deposit, and sign the first papers,"

"But, we were hoping to move in this summer and decorate,"

"Oh yeah , you can do that... you just won't own it till about November."

"You are kidding, you mean we can decorate and move our stuff in, and yet we won't actually own it for months?" I was incredulous.

" Yeah, but it's OK , 'cause if you pay a big enough deposit, they have to pay you back double, by law if they back out, and I don't think they can afford to do that - so it'll be fine!"

There was no other way, we just had to trust Jeff's judgment.

When we had sold our first cottage in Nailsworth to a friend, our solicitor nearly had a fit when we said that Clive was staying in the cottage for just one night before contracts had been exchanged. He implied that we must be mad, and he said that legally, he was 'not listening'.

So, at the beginning of August we packed the car up to the roof. We took tools, tins of paint, clothes, a load of books, some paintings for the walls, a tent, camping chairs, and a camping stove. We needed enough supplies for a month, in case we had to live outdoors, and also things to make the place feel like a home if we were able to go indoors.

All through France, we waited for a text message from Jeff, to say that our new Italian bank had received our money from the UK. Fortunately the bank manager was Alessia's brother-in-law so communication was straight-forward. The money should have gone through without a hitch but there was still no news from Jeff by the time we were more than half way through France.

We couldn't bear it any longer, so we stopped at the services in Dijon and phoned.

" Oh hi Fiona, yeah we've got the money safely, didn't you get my text? Well it was definitely sent," Jeff was still not flustered, "That means someone else has got my text saying that sixty-five thousand euro has been successfully transferred from their account to a bank in Italy... Oh dear, that'll be a bit of a shock!"

The meeting at the solicitor's office in Ancona was quite formal, as one would expect. Everything was read twice, once in Italian and once in English, for our benefit . The hi-tech office was packed with people, Jeff and Alessia were there, also the vendor's daughter and husband who owned one half of the building; and the five sisters, vendors for the other half; apparently the two sides of the family hadn't really got on for some time. The building was legally split into two separate houses rather than apartments. The five sisters had been brought together from as far away as Paris and Switzerland. It was a legal requirement that every living beneficiary must turn up to sign.

The sisters were all in their sixties with a fair amount of faux leopard or tiger skin and bling about them. I couldn't help noticing how often they tucked into the complimentary sweets in the middle of the Arthurian-sized round-table. A multitude of rings and jangling bracelets glinted in the light from the large office window as they dived into the sweety bowl.

Italians are renowned for their red tape in daily life, but the legal side of the culture is something else. The others around the table seemed to be happy to sign endless forms. There were six or seven full-name signatures on each form and piles of forms because of all the sisters involved, but they seemed to be enjoying themselves. There was a party atmosphere.

After ten minutes, I was starting to wilt. My signature was varying so much, I think anyone could have stood in for me and not a single false eyelash would have been batted. Eventually, the piles of forms and deeds were stacked on the table in front of us, resembling a paper henge. The efficient young lawyer lent forward, in his designer suit, to start the handshakes over the table. Soon it became a complicated lattice-work of humanity.

Handshakes turned into long-lost grasps of friendship. Which in turn, became hugs of passion... encircling the table in pairings of buxom bodies, it was like a primitive rite. The intermingling of all those animal prints reminded me of a Fauvist poster for a zoo. Some of the sisters hadn't been speaking for decades before this event. It seemed to be an occasion that had opened up diplomatic relations between the relations. Excitement and happiness was soaring and was made even better by the distribution of the quite modest cheques (or maybe they were just on a sugar high from all the confectionary!)

Anyway, we took the keys in the emotionally charged atmosphere, and thanked Jeff and Alessia once again for all their hard work.

" You are absolutely sure that we can decorate, and do anything we want, aren't you, Jeff?"

" Yeah, Freddie, no problem, just have a good time in your new home."

(And our faith in Jeff was proven to be valid, because we had no problems with our new part ownership).

I just couldn't believe that there would have to be a repeat match on the same ground, (or office) in a few months time. The whole thing would be finalised, and then we really would own the house. Never mind, we were heading west on the dual carriageway. The road was sign-posted, exotically, to Roma. I had the keys to a small part of Italy in my pocket... well a portion of that small part anyway!

As we climbed the hill through Castello and on to San Giovanni all thoughts of whether or not we really owned the house completely evaporated - In fact, I don't think the legal implications of going into our part-owned house and taking a sledgehammer to it (metaphorically speaking) ever entered my head again . So we drove on in a state of elation. We had achieved our goal, our mission was complete. After months of wishing and hoping, our ribboned scroll had come up trumps!

We glimpsed the house through the trees as we drove past the cemetery. The grey render was just visible amongst the dense foliage. It was the very first time that I had driven down the track, it was now so overgrown that I had to stop twice to pull away fallen branches.

We had finally arrived. This was the moment of triumph, the fulfilment of our hopes, it was time to thrust the flag into the summit of our fantasy... But this was not what I had expected - someone had substituted my dream-home for what now stood in front of me.

The house was buried deep in brambles, ragged grass and thistles. It looked completely overgrown and abandoned. The picture that I had stored in my mind for five months did not now compute. Nature had tossed in a wild card; it had simply replaced the stark snow of March with a spiky and impenetrable jungle.

I shuddered in disbelief. I knew there wouldn't be 'roses around the door,' but I hadn't expected brambles. In my dreams throughout the months of waiting, it had become a place to potter and relax. My head had been filled with slightly out-of-focus pictures of an idyllic Italian house surrounded by well-cut lawns and cypresses. It was supposed to be somewhere to mingle the pleasures of decorating, with lying in a hammock... maybe even indolently eating figs. Or a place where, before a light luncheon, I would sketch the distant view, possibly even wearing a Panama, having effortlessly just put up a shelf or hung a picture. Small tasks accomplished with ease whilst wallowing in sun and prosecco.

What I saw in reality was an awe-inspiring amount of hard work. DIY unravelling like a never ending Ikea instruction leaflet into the MDF dust of future decades.

I tried to look for positives... yes, there were figs - lots of figs, most of them rotting and stinking in the tangled undergrowth. And there, under the largest fig tree, stood the shed... the one that in my mind had become a wonderful studio but was now completely engulfed by a tangle of very unaesthetic foliage. It was barely visible through a matted mess of huge curling fig leaves and fallen plaster. And the view, probably the thing that I had been looking forward to most of all, now had to be picked at in tiny glimpses between the densely-leafed trees. At garden level, the feeling of being on the edge of a panorama had changed to that of being in a small clearing in a forest.

Not only that; the render on the house seemed to be far more cracked and grey than before. Great chunks were hanging off, channelling any rain into the inside. The shutters too, looked more warped, unfitting and rotten than I remembered. How was it possible for a house to deteriorate so much in just a few months ? Even trying to create an outside space big enough to plonk a deck chair on was going to take years, let alone to have a lawn on which to stroll at sun-down, admiring the distant vista. I think I was completely floored by the cruel warping of my fantasy. Was it too late to back out?

However, to her credit, there was not one moment that Fiona seemed the least bit fazed by it all. As we hacked our way to the door, She just kept saying, " oh... isn't it wonderful... gosh look at the figs, it's fantastic... I can't believe it... wow, it's like a secret garden... and look at that view, oooh !!"

"Eh?" I muttered to myself, " How can you see the ruddy view?"

With such a mammoth task ahead of us, it was going to be tough just uncovering a starting point in the undergrowth, let alone seeing anything else.

But Fiona's positive attitude was unwavering as we opened the door;

" Now that's strange," she said, " this room is a completely different shape from how I remember it. I was going to put a work surface there to divide up the sitting area from the kitchen area, but there's nowhere like enough room... never mind."

"Wha... what ?" I thought, is that all you've got to say.... what about the crap of three generations lying elbow deep on the work surfaces.

I kept quiet... I do love Pollyanna's positive attitude!

My memory had also altered the size and shape of every room. How easy it must be to pick the wrong person out of an identity parade, if a memory can distort such trivial things in just five months. I had even taken a video of the house in March, and I'm supposed to be visually trained!

The house had been left mostly furnished with some quite useful things but an awful lot not. There seemed to be dunes of dusty stuff everywhere, before we could start to make inroads for our own decorative taste to be imposed, there was going to have to be a major house-clearance.

You know that feeling, when you go on holiday and even if the place is nice, it still takes a few days to settle in? It takes time to put down your own scents, to make things familiar. In our situation this feeling was exaggerated tenfold, there was going to be no quick route to making this place feel like home.

Then of course there was the other, even worse part of the house that was better just to ignore for a while. Mentally, there was no way I could take any more on board - I just resigned myself to the years of work ahead, there was no choice, no way back.

The trouble was, it was my own fault. It was, after all, me who had been hankering after a new project. I was the one who had banged on about how nice it would be to have a little 'pergola and olive tree in the sun'.

Oh, bugger ... what had I done ?

Slowly during that first daunting and lengthy day, I acclimatised to the job. I tried to take hold of the thing in my mind less as a threatening building restoration and more as a casual hobby. It was after all only a sort of 'play house'. It really should not be taken too seriously, and once we had sorted somewhere to sleep and somewhere to cook, we started to take the upper hand. By dusk I think I was coming back on side, mentally. I was amazed how quickly my mindset had been torn apart and rebuilt; in a day I had been turned from someone looking for a white feather and a way to desert, into a willing front-liner.

We had made a little encampment outside, on a bit of hard standing by the back door. It was our first stake on the new land, like a base camp; there certainly was a mountain to climb the next day. Slowly, with the help of a good camping-stove meal and lashings of *vino rosso*, we started to settle into the atmosphere of our new home. We sat in the camping chairs and became aware of our strange nocturnal surroundings. As we ate, Fiona noticed a flash of light in the bushes... then another. The darkness was being scribbled through with quick lines of fluorescence: dozens of fireflies (probably the last of the season) were darting past us, their sketches in neon leaving us a memory of their flight. The tiny insects entertained us unknowingly by giving us a light show of their mating-dances, as bright as twirling sparklers.

At the same time, the stars were appearing in clear constellations. We stared at them with the same naive delight of amateur astronomer James Ferguson who, on his way home from his Highland farm work in the 1730s, would lie on his back mapping star distances with beads on a piece of string, (he also had the romantic notion that the Sun's curving path through the heavens was like "a high road running through the stars"). The cosmos spread infinity above us too, as illuminating as a William Blake illumination from Ophiuchus and the Serpens pair in the South, right around to Cassiopeia and Polaris in the North, all inter-woven with the creamy Milky Way. The evening was packed with spectacle, an exotic cabaret, act after act, performed as a welcome to our new home.

Whilst still gazing at the stars, the asteroids were waiting in the wings, eager to perform. Being close to the night of San Lorenzo (the 10th August - night of shooting stars), the sky was soon rocketed with streaks of light... we started to keep score but soon lost count. We had never seen so many shooting stars.

This was our first night and already what we were experiencing was a very different kind of entertainment from an August evening at home. It was still hot at midnight and the cicadas and gargling toads seemed to be applauding the show, keeping us in anticipation of the next encore. Enveloped by the glories of our new world, we soaked up the warmth. Both of us understood the uniqueness of the moment. We didn't even need to talk, we were united in the thrill of discovery. Like Vespucci, Bougainville or da Gama, we were on the brink of an unknown horizon and shared the intoxication of it.

There was no need to camp, we went to bed in our chosen bedroom on the high old bed with a new mattress. We felt safe because the bedroom was cosy and even though we were anxious about the future, none of it mattered for long, it had been a long day. We needed a deep sleep to gather strength for the Herculean task ahead.

The disorientation of waking in a strange place. It always takes several minutes for the recharging brain to fully engage. This particular morning I slowly gauged how I felt about where I found myself. I had an overwhelming feeling of joy at realising...

I was in Italy - despite the thought of all the work that lay ahead.

We had left the shutters open, knowing the sight that would greet us in the morning; Arcevia, on the top of the hill in the distance, with fields gently rolling towards us through the acacias. What I hadn't thought about however, was the drama of that first sunrise. Within minutes of waking, the room took on a new colour. An agent-orange light engulfed the bedroom as the high summer sun ripped its way through the horizon, directly behind Arcevia. As violent as a welding torch, it could have burnt the top off the *Duomo* with it's sheer brightness - I had to look away for fear of grilling my retinas.

For several moments we were held floating in that radium room. Elongated shadows of the trees were splayed up the bedroom walls - strangely the shadows seemed the same tone as the light, and the space was filled with luminous violets, peaches and mauves, as though Bonnard and Vuillard had 'popped in' to decorate our bedroom whilst we'd been sleeping.

A fight was on between the sun and Arcevia; so bright was the sun that first, it cuffed Arcevia in a circle of molten crimson. Then, the town seemed to hold the sun prisoner for a minute, in an amber cell. It was a mighty tussle and the town would not let go. Time seemed to stand still as the throbbing summit appeared impenetrable.

Finally, the sun made a bid for freedom, and with an epic surge of strength it pressed itself flat, squeezed and pushed. It seemed at its most powerful as it melted away both the crest of the hill and Arcevia I looked away again as it broke through the liquified horizon. The sun was victorious for another day.

It quickly changed colour from an angry orange through pink to white, like a process of purification, as if to start the new day guilt-free. The pure white circle appeared calmer once released, and it rose quickly into a duck-egg sky. It had been freed, to begin another day of heat, and with total absolution of all past days.

Sunrise in our new home: an impressive Post-Impressionistic start to a new day.

My mantra that day was going to be Aesop's wise words when a tortoise beat a hare in a sprint; " slow and steady wins the race." I got up to make a cuppa. While the kettle was heating I made a start - I felt I had to make an inroad into the massive job, just to prove to myself it was possible. Almost without thinking, I ripped a mouldering bit of hardboard off the front of the fireplace, revealing a traditional Italian fireplace. It was a symbolic act to take control of the baying hound of work ahead. Gone were the doubts from the day before; I was a worker not a shirker. I chucked the debris through the door, making the kitchen immediately appear bigger. Two tugs for a big change, all in the time it took to boil a kettle. I took the cups of tea upstairs and rejoined Fiona in bed;

"What was that crashing noise?" she asked

"Oh just part of the kitchen being thrown outside - the transformation has begun," I said, feeling an immense sense of satisfaction that I had already started.

By the end of the first day things really looked different. The way we have always tackled decorative projects is to concentrate on one room at a time. We work until every surface, including floor and ceiling has been dealt with. If anything is left unfinished, in my experience it never gets done. Also it means that at least there is one finished space that it's possible to retreat to even if the rest of the house is still a pit. We work together as a team, knowing each others' strengths and weaknesses.I have been known as the 'Filler King' for some time now (my joinery tends to be three parts wood, to one part filler) that way jobs seem to get done quicker! I had asked Jeff if we should bring paint out with us from England, and he had said:

"Well, Freddie I wouldn't bother if I was you. They've got perfectly good stuff here. English paint doesn't seem to work as well..."

I wish I had listened. The whole kitchen was clad in pine tongue and groove. It was cramped and dark looking so we decided to paint it white. Every day during that first week, one of us gave the wooden ceiling a thick coat of British, white satin one coat paint. It looked brilliant at first. But, every following morning, we woke to find it streaked with ginger. We despaired, all that work for nothing. It was pointless and relentless. So eventually, we decided to use Italian white paint. It was the seventh, neck-twinging coat and it worked immediately. I realised that what Jeff had said had been right.

Our paint is mixed with oil, and theirs is polymer based, and the two don't mix.

That first week we were like very stupid wombats, standing one behind t'other, the one behind having its burrow constantly re-filled with earth from the digging of the one in front. Somehow we were never defeated, we just kept digging ... well painting actually. Each evening we would assess the slow progress and enjoy a meal on our camping stove under the shooting stars.

By the end of the first week one room had been rejuvenated. Our persistence had paid off. Even a heavy wooden dresser had been cut in half, painted white and the top half hoisted up onto legs, to create a work-surface underneath. The cast iron range had been man-handled by just the two of us. It was heaved and dragged on tree-trunk rollers like a pyramid stone, down to the *cantina* (where it still lives to this day).

Only the gas cooker and seven dwarfs sink remained unchanged after a week. Now, if we stood with our back to them and closed one eye, the room looked complete. It was basically white except for the window frame which we painted green. All the other furniture was painted turquoise.

Now there were lamps in the corners, paintings on the walls and books on the new shelves. With the addition of music it looked and felt like home.

The first tool we bought for the garden was a petrol strimmer. I love gardening with a strimmer. I think both at the chapel and in Italy, it is the most used tool. Weeds just don't stand a chance once you have one, it's almost unfair. After a couple of times around the grassy area (not yet a lawn) between the house and the view, I had won the battle.

A passable garden of bumpy grass was achieved in a matter of hours. I could see that this place one day had a chance of looking, if not beautiful, then at least tamed.

So seven days had gone by. We had a room to sit in, and a garden where we could sit in our camping chairs and squint through the trees at the view. Thinning the trees would have to wait until the autumn. I had the perfect excuse to not begin clearing the trees yet: it's not wise to use chainsaws in the summer, because of the fire risk.

Every tiny task seemed to throw up new problems to solve - a daily hurdle race made worse by our lack of decent Italian. We had to go all the way to Bologna (a five hour round trip) on the motorway, to pick up a sink. The journey itself is on one of the scariest stretches of road I have experienced. Every time we've been along that route we've almost had an accident. For some reason drivers behave like maniacs, even though numbers of the latest casualties are posted on signs as you join the motorway.

This time we were nearly wiped out by an enormous lorry

wheel; it flew in an arc towards us from the opposite carriageway. I could tell by its trajectory that it would (probably) miss us if I slowed down. It bounced only a couple of tyre treads depth from our front bumper. I watched in the mirror as the wheel came to a spinning-top halt on the hard shoulder.

Trying to find somewhere that sold a *bombola* (gas cylinder) for the gas cooker was worse than the search for the 'Holy Grail'. It took weeks to track one down. Miles of driving around the area, slowly zoning in on the target until we were able to pounce. We asked in every shop we went into in Sassoferrato but people either didn't understand us or didn't know. We even found the one person within a ten-mile radius who spoke a bit of English but, helpful as she was, she didn't have the *bombola* 'knowledge' we desired.

Eventually, we managed to pick up the scent on the edge of town and homed in on a pet-food shop - yes, a pet-food shop. The tops of the gas bottles were just visible behind huge bags of dried *pasta*..... that's *pasta* for dogs!

We had lived this kind of *al fresco* lifestyle before, and then it had been even more demanding, when we lived in the garden shed: the 6' x 4' space was our home for six months while our first cottage was being renovated. It was good training for coping with living rough. We tried to make the inside of the shed as aesthetically pleasing and comfortable as possible; We painted it white inside and put all our books on the shelf. The walls were pinned with postcards, small poems and primitive drawings about our predicament covered any gap, like cave art.

Long after we'd lived in the shed, we climbed a thirty-foot ladder to see a cave in the Catalan region of northern Spain near Tortosa, (we were taken to this place by a local and it seemed all the more special because it was a secret that wasn't available to all). It was a site off the tourist trail and not well known. On the cave walls there were the marks of early Homo sapiens. The Paleolithic drawings on the cave were just like our doodles on the shed's walls. (Neanderthal people, the Chatelperronians, were even earlier inhabitants of Catalonia so if they had an artistic streak it may even have been their work). Anyway, it was a direct link through time. It was amazing that we had come up with the same solution, both for filling a space and for filling boredom. Scrawled across the cave walls were stick-figure drawings of people and animals drawn in charcoal, identical in every way to our drawings on the little shed walls (even stranger in the cave drawings; one of them appeared to be wearing skis!).

In the shed, we slept on the floor with our dog and cat. The door was left ajar to stick my feet out... not because of the smell, but because I didn't quite fit. To increase the legroom we made what we called the 'conservatory'. It was a piece of plastic sheeting flung over the opening. Fortunately for us it was a relatively dry summer, but in late September we were evicted by the weather when the roof blew off in a fierce storm. The shed was flooded by the deluge and sadly, many of our most treasured books were ruined.

Our lifestyle in Italy had already surpassed life in the shed by the end of the second week.

By the end of the third week we were planning to 'entertain'!

I had been mentally savouring the erection of a pergola for so long that it was, in my mind, to be the do-it-yourself climax. So having to knock it together and make a table in a day was not what I had planned. (I have since been informed by our Italian friend Paula that a pergola is only a pergola when it holds up a vine, so now we don't know what to call what I built).

We were just ripping through the work, and it was becoming like one of those ghastly doing-up house programmes on the TV. We were so tuned in to achieving our goal; filler was barely dry before it had disappeared under several coats of Italian paint. Actually the DIY bit is a bore, especially to others, but the end product is usually worth the concentrated effort.

It seemed appropriate that Peter and Richard should be our first guests. It was also the first viewing for them since we'd arrived for the summer. As they came down the track, the finishing touches were still being made. One would have thought the Queen was coming, as we preened the table to create a setting for what appeared to be a casual supper. We were exhausted but happy to have reached a position to be able to return the boys' hospitality in our own Italian garden and under our new non-pergola.

It was an unforgettable evening of warmth and relaxation. All the stress of the arrival and the weeks of work had brought us to this satisfying position. Is there anything more enjoyable than sharing food, wine and good conversation with old friends in the mellow heat of a starry Mediterranean evening? Despite the hastily made "wooden , potentially vine-carrying structure", it was a kind of completion, like a public untying of the ribboned scroll.

Our daughter Meri came out in the last week to see the house for the first time. Her only view of it so far had been from our first video. It was, after all, her decisiveness that had brought us here. As she walked around the edge of the garden, she bent down and picked something out of the rough grass.

" Wow... wicked... look !" she shouted.

" I've found a four-leafed clover...no, not one!" she bent down again, and again, "I've got four. Four, four-leafed covers!"

Is that super lucky, or do they become unlucky in bulk, who knows?

Meri was with us once again when we returned in November. It seemed only right that she should be present at the moment when the house became legally ours. At least if they wanted it back now, they would have had to have put up with our decor!

When we landed in Ancona airport, it was bitterly cold. It started to drizzle as we reached the hire car. Our first visit in March had been chilly, and snowy but the weather had been tempered in my memory by the promise of spring and even with sunshine - now this precociously icy November wind seemed intent on cutting us in half. I reminded the girls how in the summer I had noticed these bizarre little signs next to the road showing a frost symbol - there was even one with a car skidding off a road. They seemed incongruous if not downright funny when driving along in temperatures up in the forties but as my hand shook with cold as I directed the remote fob to open the car the weather felt ominous.

As we drove inland, the drizzle turned stickier on the windscreen - it became harder to wipe off. By the time we'd started to climb up to Arcevia it had turned into lumps of snow that hit the car with ominous intent. It was starting to stick to the fields, the branches of trees and the edges of the road and was already partially obscuring the snow warning signs. We pushed on, eager to get to the house before we became bogged down. We just managed to climb the road to Castello. From this point, we normally have our first thrilling sight of the house, but we couldn't even see twenty metres in front of the car. Driving had become mesmerising; it was now like watching a tumble-dryer filled with cotton-wool balls. But it was also incredibly beautiful. The fresh snow had cleansed the landscape like a layer of thick white Italian paint. Everything could be seen with a renewed childlike vision; it was a new planet waiting to be explored, and every bit as thrilling as waking to snow on Christmas day, when you're five.

I stopped the car to take a photo. All edges were rounded with the glistening impasto. Meri had fallen asleep when it had been raining, so she awoke to this smothered shock of a world. We all got out of the car. I photographed an old shed with a comical meringue of fresh snow topping it. The roof could take no more, snow was theatrically rucked in blue swags around the edges, awaiting its curtain call. In fact the whole snowscape was exaggerated and it reminded me of the film *Dr. Zhivago* where appar-ently, cinemas turned the heating down to add to the overall wintery effect. This snow too was like the creation of a film studio rather than reality, it was as though someone had gone berserk with a snow machine.

Only half a mile now, and we'd have made it..." hurrah !"

Then the reality dawned on us: the next morning we had to be in Ancona for the signing - the other sisters were all already there. After all the fussing to get everyone to turn up, it could be us who let them down. How ironic.

I carried on driving towards the village as Fiona phoned Alessia.

" You don't think it's a good idea? Oh, OK, well if you can do that, it would be great, thanks Alessia." She switched off the mobile.

"We'll have to turn back... Alessia says it hasn't snowed down by the coast for fifty years, so if we can get down there we'll be fine. She's going to book us into a hotel in Aguliano, which is only a few miles from Ancona."

By the time Fiona had finished talking, I had reached the village. It was only a couple of minutes to the house and its log-burning cosiness. But we had to turn around... if only we owned the place properly we could enjoy this wonderfully picturesque scene from the windows, so near and yet too far for us.

It wasn't to be, so reluctantly, I skidded the car round on full lock under the white church of San Giovanni, which was sitting on its alpine mound. We headed back the way we'd come, manoeuvring as best we could down the hairpin roads. The verges were already banked up with thick snow, like the Cresta-run, gleaming white and sparkling in the headlights of the car. It had all happened so shockingly quickly.

We headed back downhill towards the coast. What had seemed beautiful a moment ago was now becoming a landscape of danger. We crawled past cars that had shunted into each other, some had been left abandoned where they had ground to a halt. Some had slithered off the unmarked sides of the road, while others were left like the poles or gates in a ski slalom in the middle of the road which we slowly manouvered around. Somehow our little hire car just kept going.

The run from the airport is normally fifty minutes, but at this crawling pace it was going to take hours. We passed a van which four men who looked like priests were pushing it out of a snowy ditch. Where was Divine help when they needed it? They must have been praying for a gritter, or at least the miracle of a four-wheel drive? (It reminded me of the surrealist film by Brunuelle, where a dead donkey is being dragged by a priest.)

We dropped in altitude from Arcevia but there was no let-up in the appalling conditions, and now it was getting darker and the snow was coming down so thickly it felt vindictive, making driving within the road's invisible edges even more hazardous. Slowly we headed for the coast, the dual-carriageway had become one slow, slushy lane heading East. As we turned off for Aguliano there was no sign that the snow was abating. " but it never snows near the coast "... Alessia had promised .

The small town is built on a hill rising out of the coastal plain. As we approached, there were lots of abandoned cars at the foot of the slope; people had obviously decided that if they wanted to get to work the following morning, they had better leave their vehicles where they had ground to a halt at the bottom of the hill . A car in front of us had chains on its wheels and took the slope up to town with ease, until it met another coming down the hill sideways, completely blocking it's way. So we decided to stop too. I parked as safely as possible, then wheeled the heavy suitcase up the slippery incline. It felt as if we were on a polar expedition; every few minutes I had to stop to kick away the mini-snow balls that gathered under the wheels.

I had not seen snow this deep since the winter of 1963, when I lived in Brecon: I remember seeing the eight-foot drifts on the Heads of the Valleys road when they towered either side of our Austin A70 and being terrified that the steep-sided waves of snow might break over the car at any moment. It was so cold that winter that I was able to walk on the frozen River Usk, and I also remember my father dropping his car keys outside the garage door on Boxing day - he didn't find them again until St. David's day (1st March), when the snow eventually melted.

After we had booked ourselves into the hotel, Fiona and I were ready to settle down, have a hot bath and just relax. Meri was having no such thing;

"Come on guys, let's go out," she said, "I've never seen snow like this."

So out we went, resigning ourselves to the fact that we may very well be stuck here for a few days, so might as well make the best of it. We had, after all, tried our hardest to get to the coast, but it now looked very unlikely that we'd get to Ancona the next day.

We stepped into the cold air and at last the snow had eased a little. The town was like an over-iced Christmas cake. Snow had coated the elevations of ancient buildings, picking out the detailing. On the front of the church, where the mouldings and pediments were visible even in the dimness, everything appeared to have been highlighted with a luminous marker-pen and it glowed in the dusky light.

Around the other side of town, children sledged down any available slope, on trays or even bin-bags as impromptu sleighs. They hurtled down the traffic-free roads, totally oblivious of pedestrians - were they training for the Bologna motorway later in life? The whole town reverberated with the the sound of excited, trilling children. From the edge of the town, the land fell away in a Breugelesque manner. The scene was peppered with figures in primary- coloured clothing. People were mere dashes of red, blue and yellow against the white, indulging in snowy activities and disappearing into the purple-misted distance. In the fading light, trees stood out as matt silhouettes, a curtain of black lace over the fields.

Having been told that the evening meal was served at seven,

we thought that meant they started serving at seven and one could turn up at any time after that, but when we entered the packed dining room at about twenty-five past seven, the brightly lit room was full of truckers and travelling salesmen, most of them stranded like us. As we walked between the tables they all looked up and glared at us. They were evidently all at the same stage of their dinners. We had unknowingly committed a cardinal sin... we were late for food.

The waitress took a long time to forgive us. She plonked course after course of the no-choice, set-menu in front of us. By the time we reached the grappa, I think we had brought her round, yes, we'd had to grovel, with lots of apologetic humouring and oodles of praise for the noodles, but she eventually managed a smile.

We felt very foreign - It was horrible, like not knowing the ropes at a new school. This was something we were going to have to get used to; in our part of Italy there is still very little tourism. They have no concept of what it's like to be from another culture, so they make few allowances for any behaviour that differs from their very conservative way of life.

We still get stared at a lot - we are aliens - even when driving in an Italian number-plated car (on their side of the road), they stare they just know we're not one of them. They are so ungeared-up for foreign visitors, that although there is a tourist office in Arcevia they only speak Italian.

Looking out of the hotel window at first light, I couldn't see any movement at all, it was very quiet. However, squinting into the distance, out across the white plain, eventually I could make out a thin black line; a cleared road. Then I started noticing the occasional movement of cars, there were little headlights lighting the slush on the verges.

" It's OK, it looks like we might be able to go. They must have been working through the night... just so that we can get to Ancona, for the signing !"

The lawyer, now in a rust-coloured woollen suit, welcomed us into his warm office. It really was like deja vu. The sisters were sitting exactly where they had been months before, and they were still nibbling on the sweets... had they been there all this time? The only difference was that now they were wearing faux Leopard and Tiger fur and 'bling ... and shoulder pads, has the fashion come back in ?

Anyway, Meri proved to be a positive distraction; I think they were glad to see that young people would be enjoying their house, too. They were all over her, plucking at her clothes and hair ooing and aaring. It was great, we just passed unnoticed and got on with the final signing.

With everything completed, another bundle of cheques was eagerly grabbed from us. Jeff and Alessia introduced us to the *geometra* (a cross between an architect and surveyor) who had been responsible for a great deal of the sorting out and registering of boundaries: "This is Signor Tortalone ,"Jeff said, " I think you might find him useful. His office is in Arcevia - I mean if you need any building work and stuff. "

Sig. Tortalone looked quite strict, but would, indeed, prove to be a bit of a godsend....

We returned to our snowy house for the rest of the week, captivated by the white blanket, visually and physically. We arrived at the top of the track and realised that it would be impossible to drive down. Our kind neighbour Edris had, however, made the perfect welcome to your new home gesture; not only had he cleared a walkable path the hundred metres down to the house, he had then carried on right around the house to the woodshed. He'd shovelled a channel through the thick snow - an exhausting task at any age, but made all the more amazing by the fact that he is nearly eighty.

It should have actually been the moment to celebrate the long-awaited ownership. Unfortunately, the party had to be postponed because Meri came down with a horrible bout of flu, (maybe the chilly snow walk hadn't been such a good idea), so she spent most of the week in bed, with a bobble hat on!

PESTS AND GUESTS

The very first friend to go and stay in the house without us being there, was JC. He's unusual because he's a Druid who works for the Ministry of Defence. I asked him once;

"don't you find it odd working for the MoD. I mean you just don't seem the type, with your beard, long hair and Homberg hat?"

"Well no, that's the whole point Freddie" he said, "I'm changing the system from the inside, man."

We asked him if he wouldn't mind doing some kind of Druidic blessing on the house whilst he was there. He agreed and performed the ritual in the garden at dawn, not on the Autumn equinox itself, but I don't think that mattered. We both feel that the Celtic or pagan way of doing things has far more resonance with where we're ' coming from' than anything else on offer. (One only has to study Mithras or pagan festivals to realise what more recent orthodox religion based a lot of its ceremonies on).

I have a vivid picture in my mind of JC being spotted by Edris as he passed down the track on the way to tend his vines, almost falling off his scooter when he glanced up to see JC standing there, arms spread to the Heavens and ' tackle-out' in the golden light of dawn. JC was probably the talk of the village, but this being an area, as I said, that the Celts lived, maybe it would have felt mystically familiar in some subconscious way.

Talking of things mystical, our most frequent guest has been Val, the Feng Shui lady. During the summer, when her place in Venice is being rented, she considers us as her country residence. Initially, she was also a great helper with the paint-brush. I know she won't mind me saying; Val has many skills, amongst which is the amazing ability to accidently conserve letters in a word. She leaves out or moves the unwanted ones to create a brand new word. The creation is a Malapropism so subtle that it seems deliberate. She's especially talented at this art when she's had a small *spritz*! Brilliant expressions can come forth without her even trying;

"Could you pass the Parmiganiano please," (did you even notice? - the join is so seamless between Parmigiano and Reggiano. It's so nearly right that you're not sure if you've heard it properly).

Or, as in texts like; "Isn't it wonderful news about Oback",

Yes, again a marvellous combi-name for Barrack Obama.

Another text read : "couldn't sleep last night... too much wind,"

Followed shortly by, a few minutes later: "I meant wine!"

Then there are the more abstract ones;

"Have succumbed to Plumbago!" Is it the plant, or some horrendous back problem? And also Trompe Louis an unexplainable

(Louis Armstrong) jazz version of Trompe l'oeil.

The other day she came up with my all time favourite when describing an up-market friend; "Oh yes, they're a very old English family you know... they came over with Norman the Conquerer!"... It takes a few moments to work out its brilliance.

She also has some other-worldly abilities; for instance, the ribboned scroll, which certainly seemed to help things along for us.

So we felt very fortunate that she was with us when, whilst helping to clear the house, she came across Luigi Tristallini's old wallet.

"I know exactly what to do with this,' she said, holding it out on top of both flat palms, like a dead gerbil. With the demeanour of an undertaker she carried it slowly, garden trowel tucked underarm, her legs moving as though she was doing a slow march at a state funeral, right to the end of the garden. She buried that tatty bit of folded buff leather with full military honours, and then did a little dance which was reminiscent of Ottoline Morrell in the Twenties, a twirling mass of abstract voile and silk.

We had all assumed that poor Luigi had passed away because he hadn't been present at the solicitor's signings and also we had come across so much medical paraphernalia in the wardrobes. Also, the cupboards were full of his stuff; we seemed to have been left with all his clothes; leather bomber jacket, easy-rider sunglasses and even platform shoes from the Seventies. We'd formed a vivid image of him as a bit of a lothario (the calendar on the stairs springs to mind again!).

So it came as quite a shock when we discovered that Luigi was alive and well, living with his daughter on the coast. Now well into his eighties, he's probably still wondering what happened to his old wallet ! Actually, I'm sure he would have been delighted with its send off. Val does everything with a flamboyant generosity of spirit!

I'm not going to list all the people who've delighted us with their company here in Italy. A few just happen to have bobbed up to the surface.

When James and Sara came to stay, it turned into an experience for them that was far from straight forward. James had frisked his own pockets just before going through security at the airport and realised, to his chagrin, that he'd forgotten the tickets. He had to drive all the way back to Gloucestershire for them, a six hour round trip, so they had to stay overnight near the airport.

The next day, tickets at the ready they went to the airport; this time the flight had been cancelled, due to a suspected terrorist threat. There were no flights for three more days. So they had nice little holiday near Stansted instead. When they eventually arrived in Ancona for their (now) miniature holiday, I spotted another potential danger for James: standing at arrivals, it's possible to see your friends feet as they arrive, under the translucent glass half-doors. It's fun spotting your chums by their footwear. Anyway, this particular day I noticed a hazard; a two-metre long piece of webbing from a suitcase was lying on the floor under the doors. We weren't allowed beyond our barrier to tidy up, so just had to watch.

"Oh no James is bound to trip over that." I said to Fi.

We watched, helpless, as two hundred or so passengers managed to casually side-step the snare-trap without any problem. Then I saw James' feet, the doors opened… he didn't see the strap, and by itself, I don't know how, it managed to climb up both his legs and hold on. He seemed to launch himself at us with both legs bound like a lassoed steer.

The most amazing part of this is that he didn't even notice it. He just shook his leg and it fell off as we all hugged. I've mentioned it to him since and he has no recollection… maybe he's just used to throwing himself at people in airports?

One of the great things about having a play house is that not only is it neutral territory but also, it's not worth going all that way for less than a week, so you really get to know your friends and more often than not that is a nice experience.

We have shared many holidays with Robin and Barbara - we had children the same ages. They came to Italy the very first winter that we had owned the house and we got snowed in again. This time good and proper, trying to eke out supplies and keep warm was fine for a bit, but when we ran out of wine, we realised the situation had become desperate. There was only one thing to do; we would have to walk around to the other side of Arcevia . We just hoped that the mini-market was open in the extreme weather conditions. There was no way of checking, so we'd just have to walk to it and hope.

The walk is a good sixteen-kilometre round trip, quite a long walk in a good weather. In snow with only traction-less wellington boots it meant an agonising and tensed-muscle hike on the slippery downhill bits, making it feel double the distance. Having reached the open shop (phew!), we had the daunting prospect of the return uphill journey with all of us carrying heavy bags of shopping. It certainly was an exhausting day-out that I wouldn't want to repeat. As it was getting dark and my knees were playing up, there were moments where it would have been easier to pack it in and let the cold do its worst. But we pushed on and it's just as well we did; we passed the hire-car parked like a frozen ice breaker ship in Frobisher Bay, it was under a dome of snow and stayed immoveable for a week. We were snowed in and completely cut off from the world and if we hadn't made the expedition, we would have had to resort to eating the cat, and drink... who knows what?

One evening that week, hunched up in front of the wood-burning stove, we were chatting about what first attracted us to this part of Italy. I was explaining that we found it reminded us of Wales, but with sun (joke)! It was snowing heavily at the time... Also how the people seemed to be physically similar to the Welsh, quite small in stature, dark complexions, etc.

"I mean look at Edris," said Fiona, " he's just like one of my uncles from up the Valleys."

"Gosh, yes - Ed Rees, it's a very Welsh name too, isn't it ?" replied Robin, completely seriously!

It's strange that all I seem to have done is relate tales of snow and frost in Italy. I suppose we just don't hear as much about it. Also the snowy days stand out in the memory. The summers are, of course, worth talking about too; most summers are endlessly hot - week after week of sunny days. It's not unusual to have a month of weather in the forties. In fact, one morning last summer, I noticed on the car thermometer it was 47' C.

With the extreme weather comes extreme everything else... plants grow twice as fast as in Britain, which is good for beans and bad for brambles. Plagues of insects or other nasties seem to be twice as virulent also; they're more frightening in size and in their general unfriendly attitude. It takes a few growing seasons to get into the swing of things, and do unto them as they would like to do unto you. It is a very different attitude from home. In England I suspect most of my generation would like to be regarded as peace-loving or on the edge of hippy-laid-backness.

However only a few months ago I was really put to the test in Chalford and was able to abide by English rules. I had been stung several times on my thumb by an angry autumnal sleepy wasp. I had disturbed it in Meri's bedroom curtains at the chapel. Wow it was painful...It burned and throbbed like a stone-fish sting. Still, this was home... I had to play by "English rules".

I located him in the curtain and gently unwrapped him so that he fell safely out through the window. I thought, "there you are old chap you were only doing your duty, no hard feelings, eh?"

By contrast in Italy I asked Edris (a gentle and kind man) what he did if he came across a scorpion. He looked at me for a few seconds. First of all I could see in his face that he thought I was a bit simple, followed by a hint of real pity. Then in one smooth movement he lifted his foot and then thrust it firmly downwards onto an imaginary scorpion. He ground it in a semi-circle on the floor - a right-footed pestle and mortar action. A tiny bead of moisture was ejected from the corner of his mouth with the pressure of turning this pest into *pesto*.

"Ooohhh" I said, rather foppishly - "Bene"

I didn't have the heart to tell him I had been brushing them gently into a dustpan and escorting them to the boundary.

In Italy at least, I have had to toughen up. If I hadn't, by now the place would be occupied by sofa-eating rats with eye patches and hornets on their shoulders; rats who would spend their days fornicating on our work surfaces and playing darts with the scorpions.

The first plague that I had to engage the new me was the hornets' nest.

I had noticed first a couple, then three or five and soon a whole stream of hornets. They had become very interested in our little shed. Their scouts had been looking for a new home. I was fascinated with the gradual increase in troop movements on the shed-front. At more or less the time that we had moved in, so had they, but their numbers were increasing. They had quite clearly realised that there was a small gap in the window frame of our shed. The interior was going to make an ideal place for a new town. It must have been much like discovering the Milton Keynes building plot.

My interest in these amazing creatures, who at this stage bore no threat to us, grew. I watched them chomp on our new deck-chairs, in order to get wood for their city. Their low, "Dornier" bomber-hum throbbed as they flew relentless missions, back and forth all day long with our wood-pulp between their mandibles.

Then one morning Fiona said sadly; "You know we're going to have to do something about those hornets, don't you? Meri's coming out in a couple of weeks and is even allergic to those little hairy caterpillars, so imagine what a hornet's sting would do to her..."

She was right, I had to do something. Even though I admired these creatures, I knew it was foolish to let them live next to the house. It was all very well at the moment whilst they were building a nest, but what would happen when it came to defending their young? It would be every man for himself and they would outnumber us hundreds to one.

"OK I'll deal with it," I said, with a surge of machismo, and grabbed the fly swat: I started walking towards the shed weapon raised - alert as a ninja.

There was one solitary hornet who looked like he was just chilling out on the door of the shed. As I got closer, he saw me - he wasn't just a casual bystander, he was on sentry duty and ready to die for his cause.

He straightened up his tiny torso until he was primed on all six hairy legs. Then, he fixed me with a truly terrifying stare. What he could see, of course, was hundreds of fly swats approaching through his compound eyes. He raised himself up on tip-toes, his abdomen and thorax expanding. He was now pumped up to double his normal size. I stopped short before he could strike... and regrouped. Well, retreated actually, pathetic fly swat wilting in my hand: I was going to have something more than a fly swat up my sleeve.

A special trip to the *Brico*, the DIY Shop, was called for. I needed to get properly tooled up. In Italy, they take pests seriously; there is a whole aisle dedicated to extermination, as British supermarkets have one alloted to different types of crisps.

The various poisons, traps and weapons ranged from, at one end, powders for very small creatures like ants or centipedes, passing through an area for vermin of various sizes, mice and rats, on to the other end of the aisle, where there were Gatling guns to take out wolves and bears, (only joking) but it was all very impresive to me!

Back in England I've been known to take a mouse, caught in a humane trap, for a little outing in the car, like some kind of treat or reward for being well behaved: I've taken the creature for miles up to an area of pleasant common land, in order to set it free. Then, I've helped the little fella settle in to the new area - like a vermin co-councillor.

Eventually, I found the very thing for our hornet problem: a huge spray can bearing warnings, in red letters, about the dangers of hornets. The can, once shaken for the right amount of time, apparently squirted a thin beam of ectoplasmic white liquid for forty feet. It sounded horrendous, but was especially formulated to deal with a potential attack from long distances, in roof spaces and the like. (Since, I've heard that if one has a nest of hornets in a loft space it's quite usual to call out the firebrigade, when our friends did, they said the big butch firemen were terrified of the hornets too!)

My battle was going to have to be planned carefully. I didn't want to end up with a 'Seige of Hornetgrad' situation, where the war could drag on for weeks or even years. A situation in which Fiona and I would have to resort to eating the deckchairs, too, because we daren't leave the house. Surprise was going to have to be my main weapon.

It said on the can to wait until night fall, when hopefully the enemy would be sleeping (and if they had a guard he would probably be dozing on duty).

It also said to wear rubber gloves and goggles. In fact, to cover every part of the body just in case - it really was doing nothing for my nerves. I made sure that I had an operational torch too. I laid out all my gear as though I was going on an Apollo Mission. The problem area in my attack plan was going to be opening the stiff, locked door with one hand while carrying the large spray can and directing the torch with the other. All this noisy action had to be executed quickly, before the hornets woke up to welcome me in their shed.

This was strictly a one-try affair so I had to get it right; I also wanted to do it as quickly as possible for the poor wee beasties sake.

I put on the outfit, looking like a cross between a 'Ghost-Buster' and someone allergic to sunlight. The pink rubber gloves were particularly un-SAS.

All too soon, Zero-Hour was here: I started to shake the can whilst still inside the house as the noise of the little ball-bearing would have roused even the most somnolant hornet. I could procrastinate no longer, my stomach churned as Fiona opened the kitchen door.

This was it.

I ran into the darkness towards the shed. My wellies squelched as I threw myself at the shed door. My pulse was pumping... I hit the guard on the door frame with my laser-beam of foam, just as he was raising his head to look at me... I fumbled with the key, trying to position it between my clumsy, rubber-gloved fingers. It kept clicking against the lock and noisily missing the hole. Then it was in, come on... twist... jolt... my shoulder shoved, and the door opened... ... it banged loudly against the inside wall.

"Sssshush", I uttered without thinking.

Quick, quick... but where were they? The torch's beam seemed to be dying already as it scanned the inside; I shook it, and it lit up to the roof briefly, then rapidly the light darted from side to side, flickering and flashing out of control. I couldn't find them and my light was running out.

Then, from behind the door... and behind me, there was a low buzzy drone, like someone starting a rusty old Vespa (which means wasp in Italian, by the way) . No time to think, I swung around and fired; the spray came out at force. I continued to hold the button down as I backed out of the door, still firing. I clawed my way out of that living hell! Feeling a bit like the ' Sundance Kid ' or ' Dick West ' firing upside down under his saddled horse, I kept shooting the stream of foam until with a last grope in the darkness I pulled the door shut. The night op. was over and I was very hyped up. I received a hero's welcome back in the kitchen.

At least the dirty deed was done.

In the morning, returning to the scene of the crime, I cautiously entered the shed; behind the door I had evidently made a direct hit because there, built into a corner, was the magnificent, partially constructed hornet's nest. It was amazing - a super-sized honeycomb structure, hanging like an inverted dome as good as Brunelleschi's in Florence, and equally unfinished (if you look at the collar of the dome). All this made from our deck-chair pulp and masticated by these small creatures to create a golden masterpiece. I felt I had destroyed the Ideal City.

I have not yet recovered from the guilt, actually, and am not proud of what I did, but because of the potential threat to Meri's safety at that time, I felt I had to do it. Did some of the Conquistadores have similar feelings, I wondered, passing the common cold on to the Aztecs? The fact is I find it hard to justify my actions and the responsibility for the extermination of this particular precociously advanced small tribe of insects lies solely with me.

Now of the hornets themselves there was no evidence. What had been left of them had been eaten overnight by another predator.

Life and death seems harsh in Italy compared to tame England.

The hornets were just the first of many such plagues, but each time another came along I became more battle hardened. In the end I could swat and spray with the best of 'em. I remember particularly the "Summer of Flies": some friends, Paul and Jane, were staying with us. They were so patient, but the invasion of flies must have made their holiday difficult. Paul even managed not to mention them in his wonderful video of the area, although I think we are caught on camera, fly swats quivering at the ready!

It had been a bad summer for flies all over Italy. Our situation was made worse by the construction of a new farm not far away from us. They had not dealt with the potential pests in the spring, when they were hatching, so it became an extraordinary fly phenomenon. It's hard not to sound like I'm exaggerating the problem but there were literally zillions of the little creatures. They covered every surface and no matter how many were 'taken out' there was another battal-ion right behind to take their place. We all know that everything is here on the planet for the delicate balance of life cycles, but what makes an unbalance like this? They don't even sting to keep you indoors - they are just plain annoying.

We wondered if there was any way of organising the system that they had introduced in China to solve the fly problem; apparently during the Cultural Revolution, there was a financial reward for people who killed ten or more flies a day. So effective was this rather capitalist way of solving the problem that flies became almost extinct. They had solved the problem to such an extent that there were no more flies, therefore no more money. So people began breeding flies to pick up the reward.

Here in San Giovanni, there was no need for a breeding programme yet. Our mission was beyond tedious. Day after day of slaughter made no inroads into the problem. The only real pleasure left in life was scoring a 'double' or even a 'treble' with the swat. Even nature-loving Fiona became reluctantly adept at the backhand squish.

I was trying to rough-render the walls of our *cantina*. I mixed cement in sloppy piles on the floor, but unfortunately it was when the flies were at their worst in the heat of August . I 'd start mixing the cement, then have stop to kill flies... then, mix... swat... mix ... swat, again and again. I was hot, sweaty and literally covered in them. Meanwhile the two butcher's-shop style fly zappers would be killing as many as they could just to try and help. Then I would mix a bit more cement and kill more flies, and so on and on all day every day. It was a war of attrition and was unwinnable. The finished render job looked just like a school pudding ... spotted dick!

After a couple of particularly fly-ridden days at the end of the rendering job, I filled a shoe-box to the brim with dead flies - just a day's tally. We took them to show sig. Tortaloni, to see if he could do anything to help .

I placed the box in front of him on his desk.

His eyes lit up; he thought it was a present for all the work he' d done on the house.

Just before he opened it, Fiona and I managed to blurt out *"Non è un regalo!"* (it's not a present). But he still jolted backwards with shock and total revulsion at the sight of a million dead flies... (although it did look remarkably like a bumper box of raisins!)

He said nothing more. We left it in his capable hands. After all, he had been involved in the design of the new farm, so we assumed that he would have a word with them. And presumably he did because since then, we have had only a 'normal' number of flies.

Meanwhile, during that Summer, we knew there was one other thing we could do to help stop the fly problem, indoors at least; so we made our way down Corso Mazzini to see the "Blind Man".

The man in question was a picture-frame maker in Arcevia. He also made and fitted the frames for fly-blinds, hence his nick-name. He was amazingly efficient; we had thought the chances of having blinds made for the current problem was very unlikely. I thought we could look forward to having them done for the following summer. We had girded our swots for the 'fly war' to continue all that year.

Amazingly however, his son came around that very afternoon to measure up all the windows. He then asked if we would like them on Thursday or Friday.

"What this week?" I said, in disbelief.

"*Si, certo!*"

So quickly was the job done that I arranged to pay the following week. I was only able to draw out a small amount of cash daily from the cash machine and it was going to take quite a time to get all the money.

They agreed that was fine. However, when the fly blinds had been fitted and they all looked brilliant, I was taken aback when the fitter came towards me with his hands outstretched, palms upwards, making a Fagan-like grasping gesture.

" Money, money," he said ... "money, money..."

"Gosh", I thought, "how vulgar."

"Now look here," I said, " we had an agreement that I could pay later next week."

" no , no, money, maney ... mani, ... mani," he said, looking pleadingly at his hands.

What he was actually saying gradually became clear as it metamorphosised in my mind from money to *mani*... hands. His hands were covered in silicone gel from sealing the frames in.

My translation skills had let me down again.

"Oh, you mean... *mani* ... your hands... you want to wash your hands ? Sorry."

The fly-blinds were excellent, and it now meant the windows could be left open day and night. A through draught, even on the hottest days, without a single fly, moth or mosquito.

We have also had the mini plagues of insects that only last a few hours; plagues of ants are easily dealt with - just a few puffs of powder and it's all over. Others can seem slightly more dramatic, like the day we came back home in late August to find the whole fireplace black and crawling with thousands of flying ants, apparently it was the 'day of flying ants,' when they all hatched at the same time, which this time was down our chimney. When this happens there's a frantic five minutes of spraying and flailing of swats and then vacuuming. Everyone available of killing age is brought into service until every last invader is seen off.

Our friends from Gloucestershire, Jane and Howie, who are always fun company and enthusiasts for life in general live a rural life at home. They have kept chickens, ducks and other types of animal life but I think that our rural life in Italy was a bit too 'rural' for them. Howie is a bit of a baby when it comes to snakes and scorpions (understandably, perhaps !)

They stayed at our house whilst looking for a place to buy in Le Marche and Jeff and Alessia showed them a few rural dwellings in our area. I think it was more the threat of the unknown, rather than seeing anything particularly creepy crawly at our house, but one visit to our place made them decide that a country property was not for them. In the end they opted for a more urban and urbane lifestyle which suited them better. They bought a luxurious apartment in a *palazzo* in the beautiful city of Ascoli Piceno in the southern Marche. We occasionally stay with each other and it means we all benefit from having time in both city and countryside .

As for the scorpions and snakes, they are a pretty rare sight. The more lived-in a place is, the less likely one is to see them. The small black scorpions (Euscorpius italicus) can be found all over Italy and the Mediterranean in general. Whilst it's sting is not lethal, it is said to pretty painful; our friend Jill was stung by a scorpion in her own house in Italy, when it fell (or jumped !) off a beam, down into her cleavage. She said the pain was only equivalent to a bee sting, her husband Alan was stung 'down below' by one of those innocuous looking centipedes that was taking shelter in his underpants. He said the pain was worse than childbirth (he is a doctor, so he should know)... and the swelling apparently was similar to pregnancy too!

I've seen the snake three times in five years. It is pretty impressive; it's sleek, black and over a metre long. It's also very fast. Holding out an olive twig of friendship and with our need to anthropomorphise, we've called him Cecil (It could well be a Cecilia though). He's not venomous and is really the over-inflated black equivalent of a British grass snake. Apparently, the snake species is called a ' Western Whip '. If it could be renamed ' Walnut Whip ' it might be viewed more affectionately. As D.H Lawrence observed in his poem about a " Snake " in Sicily " black snakes are innocent, the gold are venomous", we feel our's is big, black and so far, innocent.

Cecil's taken a fancy to our *cantina* in the springtime, probably for some nesting reason. Fiona had a horrible shock when she accidently disturbed him; he was sleeping, draped along the top of the cantina door. Silly boy! Fortunately, Fi was carrying a basket of washing so kicked the door open and poor Cecil had an abrupt awakening; he fell to the the floor in a heavy writhing, slump. Had Fi opened the door with her hand, as she usually did, the snake would have fallen on her head instead of at her feet... I've had to put nails along the top of the door to stop him using it as a bed.

Another regular guest whom we feed daily, once she discovers we're here again, is a shy tabby cat we have named 'Bella'. We aren't sure how old she is or whether she was once owned by Luigi, but we think she's also middle aged. Every year, when we arrive for the summer, (being middle-aged she is no doubt , like us, looking for new adventure) because, there is always a kitten ... or two, nesting underneath our studio/ shed. She tentatively introduces them to us during our stay, not letting us get too close. However, by autumn she's sent them away. They get dragged by the scruff of the neck to the village so she can concentrate, once more, on getting all the food from us, without having to share it. His eyes are too close together and his ears slope backwards at a very shifty angle. His back legs are spread wide apart and he walks with a low-life gait. We call him ' Bollocks ' for two (all too) obvious reasons. He looks totally untrustworthy ... shame on Bella. She seems to be very impressed by him, although she could definitely do better. However, it really is none of our business who she has as a mate. Nor is it up to us to take Bella to the vet when she's ill. Or even worry if she doesn't turn up for supper. She's the perfect pet and we have a mutually respectful and distant relationship. She doesn't like to be touched, but likes to be near us. We are pleased to see her when she turns up, and we presume she feels the same. She brings us a chewed lizard or mouse as her kind of thank you for the food we leave out for her.

Who could ask for more?

At home in England, this is the first time in thirty years that we have been pet-free. We really enjoyed our era of animals, but now that there are no young at home, we are enjoying the freedom of being able to just pop out to Italy without the hassle of booking catteries and kennels. Alas our garden is a bit like a pet cemetery and there's no more space, not for a Gerbil or even a wallet!.

Our first pet was called "Teasel", a very black and spiky cat. Pre-children, he was a surrogate child and really much brighter than the pair of us. He knew exactly how to wind us around his little dewclaw and if ever we upset him in any way, he would take his revenge. I think he must have been a thespian in a previous life, such was his sense of melodrama and timing. Once we wronged him by not coming home for the weekend. David was living with us at the time, so he was being fed, but that was not enough; to demonstrate his displeasure at this perceived abandonment, he peed in both Fiona's new shoes. An equal amount in each shoe. Which means he must have stopped mid-flow in order to move his bottom - surely the work of an evil genius (with amazing bladder control).

I think lavatorial was his genre of humour, because another

time, when we were trying to impress our new landlord by showing him the newly decorated sitting-room, Teasel scrambled up the chimney in front of us all, paused for a moment, then crapped from a great height with superb dramatic aplomb. We were all left speechless, standing over the steaming pile. The landlord turned around and left, without a word. I don't think he had ever witnessed anything so appalling and he was probably in shock. It certainly didn't reflect well on our home-making skills...

Teasel was particularly cross whenever he had to be given a worming tablet. He was a master of deception and even though we would butter the thing or coat it in food, it could take up a good part of an evening, trying to exhaust him before he noticed us tiring, as we both attempted to hold him down - one to stroke his throat whilst the other tried to prize open his man-trap jaws. We would go through dozens of aborted swallows; he'd slyly hold it in his gums until it came squirting out on whichever side there was no fielder. Eventually, even he would get fed up of the game and would appear to take the tablet quite easily, almost opening his mouth to show us and say "Aaaah... there see, all gone ... honest," He'd jump down from the table and we'd have a sense of relief and achievement. We'd actually won this time. Then, just when he was too far away to catch, he would eject the tablet with considerable force. It would ricochet like a small calibre bullet off the floor boards. Then he'd run.

After one such battle of wills, when for once we really had won, we worried for days how he would get back at us. He built the tension by acting normally. But I knew his twisted mind was waiting for just the right moment to strike. It was almost a relief when I came across a rat in our bedroom. Only a rat this time, that's fine, I thought, I can cope with that... Over its middle, Teasel had carefully draped the wardrobe curtain. It was arranged so artfully, splayed out on either side with a professional stylist's flair. The rear end of the rat, although quite shocking, was unmarked and the tail had been laid out with a long pink flourish. Slowly, I pulled the curtain back, to reveal the hideously chewed and theatrically hacked front end. It was pure, deliberate sadism and Sam ' Peckinpaw ' couldn't have made it more gory. How is it possible for a cat to lay a curtain so immaculately over a dismembered rat? Did he have help? What the hell was going on in our tiny cottage - was he part of some kind of feline coven? I looked around; maybe he was watching, like some weirdo, from a crack in a thumb-latch door. Even worse... was he getting some kind of prurient pleasure just imagining my shock when drawing back that curtain?

In our tiny cottage there was no escape from our over indulged 'boy-cat'. He had taught himself to open all the thumb-latch doors by simultaneously jumping and swinging, two paws applying just the right amount of pressure. Pre-children, of course we spoilt him; he slept between us with his head on the pillow. He even lay across the back of my neck and shoulders, hanging as limp as a scarf whilst I painted. The relationship was a bit intense - even claustrophobic. Sometimes, we needed our own space; we just had to get away - We even had to resort to hiding. Two fully grown adults being intimidated by a small fury creature... pretty pathetic really.

Our cottage was built into a bank of earth at the back. It was easy for Teasel to run up and over the roof to the front, where there were two small dormer windows, one into our bedroom and the other into the studio, so there was no escape from his demanding stare. It was all too easy for him to watch us through the upstairs windows like something from Hitchcock's 'Psycho'. He knew we were always there - after all we worked at home. We were on constant call to fulfil his every desire. Sometimes, to avoid his intense gaze, we had to pin ourselves against the wall, either side of a window. We were like special forces training for a hostage seize, and although he knew we were there, there was nothing he could do to get at us. As long as we stayed completely still, hardly even daring to breathe, we felt we could win, again. All we could see was his ridiculous inverted long-eared shadow moving across the opposite wall like *Nosferatu*. An elongated ball of fluff screaming 'meeooow' as his body went rigid with rage.

His stubby little nose was put out of joint when our friend

Clive brought us a strange puppy which Fi named Shelley (after the romantic poet, Shelley). The poor little creature was far from poetic although she did have a nervous energy associated with a troubled soul - she had already had three prospective homes that day. The last one had been in a fish and chip shop down Barton Street in Gloucester, probably where Fred West picked up the occasional fish supper. Her nerves weren't soothed that first evening, when she settled down in the little box of straw that she'd travelled in by the fire to keep her warm, because, a rogue spark spat from the fire into her straw bed. The ensuing panic and fire-drill must have made her think, "here we go again!"

Part sheltie, part whippet, she was a custom-built fidget. With her pointy paws, she conducted her life at a fever pitch like a whippety Woody Allen. She was highly strung and constantly on the move with a twitchy trigger claw. She would attack without warning - not that she was vicious, just neurotic. She absolutely adored David, but he was definitely no pet lover. He just about tolerated her and if she jumped on his lap, he would fake a strangling action. Once he went too far; he had just made himself a pale green silk T-shirt which was on his lap. She jumped up, he feigned his usual strangling motion - and she peed all over the T-shirt.

What was it about us that made our pets have such dubious toilette habits?

Where we all lived in Nailsworth, a footpath went down a steep incline at the edge of our garden, so you could watch people pass by at jugular height. Shelley was very partial to launching herself off the edge of the garden at innocent passers-by, without warning. I remember the look on the face of one jolly rambler as he descended the path to Nailsworth, having just bid us 'fare-de-well and a 'good day' ... Shelley sprinted towards him to no doubt return the felicitation, but did not stop at the boundary. She just launched herself at throat level towards the good yeoman walker, (I suppose we should have felt a glimmer of responsibility, but because she had so recently been thrust upon us, I don't think we did). Seeing the gnashing jaws heading towards him, the poor unsuspecting walker shrieked:

"B l o o d y   H e l l !" as he shot off down the hill with dear little Shelley flying passed his left earlobe in slow motion, chewing air.

She wasn't a good sleeper either. In those first years of her life, she would wander around the kitchen all night, defacating in varying amounts. Sometimes there would be thirty or forty little presents waiting for us in the morning, ranging in size from pea to pasty. They lay in patterns, like a painting made of elephant dung by Chris Ophili, all over the swirly-patterned vinyl floor. David and I turned the laborious task of picking it all up into a game; the back door was through a small lobby, and opened onto rough waste land at the back of the house. The object of the game was to flick the poo outside with a piece of hardboard. It took considerable concentration and dexterity; if Tiger Woods had been there, I don't think he would have found it easy. The flick of the wrist had to be just right in order to hurl and curl the crap accurately at the tricky angle through two doors and a lobby. It was the turd equivalent of Beckham or Forlan bending a free kick from just outside the box. A skill that had to be learnt through daily practice… sometimes it could take three or four flicks! I can't remember how we scored, maybe to get it through the doors and out was enough .

This jolly game went on for weeks. In fact until the day that the landlord called unexpectedly and stood under a 'miss-hit' that had gone unnoticed. It was just hanging on by one sticky end - like a limp saveloy, above the door. It was hard to keep a straight face as he stood beneath it and went on about the rates in a very serious voice. Fortunately it didn't fall, or the game would have been called 'the eviction game'.

Shelley had another incredible skill; she had the most magnificent soprano voice I've ever heard… on a dog. If you had her on your lap and happened to yodel or even just wheeze a little, she'd be off... leaning back into a virtuoso performance. With small head and long nose tossed back, she looked like a canine diva. Her tiny currant eyes glazed-over with the ecstatic pleasure of it all.

At that time, David shared the house, the animals, and the art. He has been around so long that he really is like part of the family. Our children have always known him as ' wicked ' Uncle David. Naming him that probably did their mental health no good at all whilst they were growing up. And what did their teachers think if he was mentioned at school?

He will readily admit that he's a half empty-glass kind of person (usually a gin one!) and is the only person I know who greets the Summer Solstice with: "Well that's it… the nights are drawing in now!" He's also renowned for his delightful observations of nature ; " look, there's one of those beautiful little blue butterflies… that lives on shit!"

Or his other cheery yule-tide saying:

"Winter comes… and everyone dies."

But when he came out to see our house in Italy for the first time after the considerable effort we'd put in, I was, vainly I suppose, expecting some kind of positive feedback if not praise. All he said when looking around the new white sitting room was; " There's one bracket under that shelf that's smaller than all the others,"And blow me down he was right. I looked under the bottom shelf, which meant getting on hands and knees bending my neck at a painful angle, then concentrating 'til the blood throbbed in my temples. There, out of sight was a slightly smaller bracket. I had put the shelves up and hadn't even noticed. David is like the building inspector from Gehenna.

He does however speak reasonable Italian, and so we asked a favour of him when we'd owned the house for about a year; our lovely neighbour Edris had come around for a coffee in the garden. We had never quite established what his wife's name was, and it was far too late for us to ask - it was becoming embarrassing, so we asked David to find out what it was, in casual conversation. Over coffee, the conversation flowed, until the right moment came; David asked, in passable Italian, " So what's your wife's name?"

Edris answered, "Edris."

"Gosh that's unusual, so you've both got the same name then," we all said, amazed.

"What do you mean, no - my name is Ido!"

So all this time (ever since he let us into the house, that first time), we had got his name wrong. Oh the shame of it. It took a good six months before we came to terms with his new identity.

The wildlife in Italy is not all to do with creatures who are waiting for an excuse to attack. It also differs from England in many positive and interesting ways; we've had the rare privilege of seeing not just one, but a pair, of circling golden eagles. They glide their way between the nesting sites in the Furlo Gorge and the national park up the road in the Frasassi Gorge. It's a privilege to be able to look down on such a huge creature from the end of our garden, and to study its broad back and mighty wingspan as it floats past with its great wing feathers fingering the breeze. And when the sun shines on its wings, or creates a golden halo of light around it, as it suddenly lifts itself with the silent ease of a towed glider to soar above us, you can see how aptly named it is.

Also, we have seen wild boar crossing the road near-by and have heard them snuffling around the garden. They sound just like farmyard pigs as they oink and squeak to their young in the early hours. In the autumn, the hunters come down our track with their guns and dogs, hoping to bag a wild boar for the pot. The gunfire echoes around the valleys from dawn. It's sensible to wear bright colours if working with trees or just rambling through the countryside at this time of the year. Because people in Italy are free to roam the countryside at will, one is quite likely to come across someone in army fatigues, lurking at the bottom of the garden. They could be hunting for rabbits or wild boar, or foraging for wild berries, nuts, mushrooms or even truffles.

We've been told that our land is perfect terrain for truffles, having an abundance of oak trees and broom growing in close proximity. We often see men and hounds going down our track, trying to hide the tell-tale narrow truffling spade behind their trouser-leg. They tend to be extremely secretive about the buried treasure. I'm sure that because we're foreigners, they think we don't know what they're up to on our land. An area where truffles are found is a precious secret that is passed down through the generations, like an heirloom. We wouldn't dream of interfering with it in any way. However, I would love to grate a bit of home grown truffle on my pasta.

There are also porcupines on the land just below. Ido said that this year, they dug up his potato crop, and he gave us a fistful of spines which resembled ancient writing quills, to prove it. He also mentioned something about wolves that we didn't quite catch. We've yet to see evidence of wolves, although late at night there have, just recently, been distant howls. (I must add here, that as a child, wolves were top of my list of terrors, once after a bad dream my parents had to comfort me, my dad said, "don't worry, the only wolves in Britain are a football team!"). They have been reintro-duced to the national park only a few miles away, so there's nothing to prevent them coming our way; now it's only a matter of time before my dreams really do come true.

If the long-legged dog fox is anything to go by, then the wolves should be impressive. I had a battle of wills with the fox twice now. Both times I've come across him standing, bold as red brass, on our lawn. He has confidently stood his ground and we've engaged in a staring contest. The score is one all at the moment.

Bird life is similar to Britain, with a few exotic exceptions. We've seen plenty of woodpeckers and jays, close up, they seem tamer. The birdsong in the spring is a spectacular cacophony, as every bird tries to out-chirp its neighbour. There is a part of my brain that tells me that this is how it used to be in our part of Britain, or perhaps I'm just in the ' summers were better when I was young', mindset. The cuckoo population could be regarded by some, (not us) as a noise nuisance here, so voluminous is their contribution to the spring dawn chorus. The nightingale too, per- haps because it sings through the night - but no, surely nobody could object to the melodious song of the nightingale? (Well actually, I remember a holiday in France, where David, even though he wasn't part of a conversation added his point of view; we were in the garden chatting, having just arrived, and I asked if anyone had been lucky enough to hear a nightingale locally. He stuck his head out of the upstairs lavatory window where he was sitting;

" Hear one? " David shouted, " that fuckin" nightingale keeps me awake every night."

A special but rare sight is the flash of yellow as a golden oriole streaks by. One morning we awoke to see a golden oriole in the acacia tree opposite the bedroom window. It shone like a golden nugget, illuminating its surroundings. We were able to observe it unseen for several minutes without moving from our bed.

Most unusual of all however is the sight of a hoopoe (in Italian an *upupa*), which we have now seen twice. Both times have nearly caused a car accident. We were driving along the infamous road for prostitutes, from Arezzo. We had just been telling David how we used to enjoy spotting the ladies at the side of the road, when Fiona almost made me crash the car when she shouted very loudly in my ear; " Look, there's one!.."

I swerved, scanning the verges in the hope of spotting one of the colourful prostitutes... but oh no.

Fiona added, ".... of those hoopoes,"

The first time we saw one was almost a fatal meeting for the hoopoe. You always expect a bird in the road to take off as you speed towards it, and normally they have the sense to oblige. In Italy however, they do seem to leave it until the last second, perhaps another test of Italian machismo! This bird, having even less road sense than normal didn't budge, it just stood on the road in front of us, forcing us to skid to a halt only inches from its ridiculous topknot.

Stupida-Upupa!

I find the Italian names for birds very appealing; *martin pescatore* for kingfisher, *cardellino* for the evidently God-fearing goldfinch, and the best of all; *pulcinella di mare* for puffin, very appropriate with its big 'Punch'-like bill.

The *upupa* is not the only bird we've come across with bad road sense, late one summer's night, when coming home from Richard's fiftieth birthday party, over the mountain *strada bianca*, we came across a flock of little owls just standing in the road. They were toasting their bottoms on the still warm gravel and standing totally motionless. They looked like little pale chess-pieces in our headlights. They didn't move so we simply had to weave carefully between them. As we passed by, one of the owls opened a huge round eye and it reflected the light-beam like a prism... owls-eyes are every bit as effective as cats-eyes to place in the middle of the road.

Even the smallest action in this very rural area has an effect in some way on the wild-life. For instance I had just hacked at a line of trees and saplings along the boundary, in order to make a hedge, and this had a knock-on effect on the fauna. Hedge laying seems to be unknown in this part of the World, certainly to one passer-by anyway; a squirrel. He was (Teasel excepted) the angriest creature I have ever witnessed in the flesh or fur. The squirrels in the Marche are particularly handsome; they are like the indigenous British red squirrels but darker, almost black, with cute tufty bits on their ears. They look like Italian soldiers when they wear those black feathered hats on ceremonial occasions.

The squirrel in question came bouncing and jumping along the row of trees along our boundary, as he had done for years. He had the same cocky confidence of a black BMW driver on the *autostrada* to Bologna, when suddenly his flow was curtailed; the next tree in line, onto which his feet normally and confidently landed, had disappeared. He slammed on his brakes at the top of the last tree in a state of furious disbelief. I could see him looking ahead, into the void. The row of trees that he had always taken for granted now only existed in his memory. He could not believe it - nothing this dramatic had probably happened to him or his family for generations. It was comparable to someone removing all the bridges over the Thames at night, without any warning or explanation. I was looking down on him from the end of the garden and felt really sorry for his predicament; I had no idea that laying a hedge would have such an unexpected consequence. For him, life would never be the same; it was his mini-nemesis time.

Slowly, he put himself into reverse gear and descended backwards - he paused at ground level and then ran up the trunk of the tree again at speed, trying to rejig his memory … but once more came to a dead halt. He simply couldn't take it in and slid backwards down the trunk, his irate claws digging into the bark. As he went down, he emitted a loud clicking noise from his throat - it was the most stressed noise ever to come out of eight inches of fluff. He took another run up… stop… slide, a lot of clicks … run, stop, slide, clicks… he did it five or six times and each time he got more angry and I'm sure was swearing at me in clicks. It was worse than stretching a chest-expander to breaking point - I could almost feel the heat coming off his distraught pelt from fifty metres away. And that ridiculous clicking noise, it haunts me even now.

Then I considered his predicament. Should I really have to bear the blame for his situation? It hadn't after all been a deliberate act of sabotage or terrorism. He really was over-reacting - he could always just walk around the gap, for goodness sake. So after a while, I thought;

"Hey squirrel... look, things change… just get over it!"

Yes, I had hardened.

RETCHING AND SKETCHING

One of the most pleasurable things on a hot day in Italy is to wander with a pad and 2B pencil, sketching, it helps you to explore an unfamiliar environment with an innocent curiosity. Creating a book of drawings of new experiences is a way of making a visual journal of discovery. It often has a freshness or spontaneity that can be easily lost in a subsequent painting. These sketches, no matter how slight, can take you straight back to how it felt at the time - each drawing is a time-whisk that stirs the memory. It's possible to remember the colours, smells and even to feel the heat of days and experiences that may have become caked to the corners of your mind. Memories and details of a holiday are easily re-lived as the pages of a sketchbook are thumbed through - it's an animated ' flick-book ' movie of small events that can reanimate the atmosphere of an entire summer.

After one particularly sketch-able day of sun, we were invited, along with Robin and Barbara's family, to supper at Giovanni and Maria's house in the Veneto. A chance to experience home cooking and local cuisine. We were staying in an ivy-covered mill which was set in an unspoilt green valley. The day had been spent baking ourselves in the July heat. We bathed and fished in the aban-doned mill pond, our bodies turning to cast bronze. By the end of the day we were all hungry, but my skin already felt as tight as a tambourine from the sun.

That evening, Giovanni proudly took us around the diminutive small-holding next to his house. Back home in England, the garden would no doubt have been laid down to grass and sur-rounded by herbaceous borders of hollyhocks and delphiniums, but in Italy it was very different; this was a serious food factory. If it grew, it was for eating, and if it moved, it was for eating also! Everything alive on that small, hot piece of land could have been sold in a market food-stall, except for the canaries (we thought). It was as though the garden was productive on three layers underground were the carrots, beets and potatoes, at ground level were the lines of garlic, onions and salad crops and all this neat produc-tivity was towered over by the high-rise population in cages; the chickens, rabbits, and canaries (kept for their beauty) were all stacked on top of each other in a vertical, living-larder.

The children enjoyed seeing all the small, caged animals, they really loved the brightly coloured canaries and spent half an hour trying to encourage the little birds to sing. Meanwhile we sat outside for aperitifs and *antipasti.* I wish now I'd held back a bit as plate after plate of tiny savoury treats were brought out.

Eventually we were taken indoors to a dining room with a roaring fire at one end. There were small pieces of meat sizzling on a spit over the heat. It was still over forty degrees outside but the fire was necessary for cooking, so if we wanted to eat, we would have to put up with the intense heat. Now I don't know about you, but I always find that being too hot is a good appetite suppressant. I was rapidly losing my appetite by degrees (of course having already filled up on the *antipasti* didn't help) and in that stuffy heat, even breathing was difficult.

We seated ourselves down as far away from the fire as we possibly could. First came the *pasta* course and Maria brought in a massive lasagne. I love the dish and this was truely exceptional, the cheese topping perfectlybrowned and melting over the sides of the huge oblong pan. There was enough food for at least twenty people but we were only six adults and four children.

The awful thing about being brought up to be relatively polite is that it's hard to refuse something so generously presented, even if your stomach is saying 'stop'. We all tucked in helping after helping and I must say we made a pretty good attempt at clearing the whole dish. Just as the last mouthfuls were about to disappear, Maria appeared with an identical lasagne… We'd made such a fuss of the first one, that she felt we needed more.

We had to at least try to make inroads into number two, just for Maria's sake. *Pasta* with cheese must be the edible equivalent of floor screed. I could feel it filling in holes that food had never reached before, just levelling off as it touched my heart. Delicious as it was, my stomach was distended to its maximum capacity and in the distance I could see the spit-roasted noisettes of meat still turning in front of the fire. There was no way I could eat any more.

But we had to. I felt like one of those contestants in an 'eat-as-many-haggises-as-you-can-in-ten-minutes' competitions. With no break in the feeding frenzy, the little joints of roast meat were being slid to the end of their skewers and plopped onto serving dishes in steaming piles. Never before had food been so undesirable. I told Maria that I could only manage a small portion. She ignored me. I'm male and she was Italian, t herefore 'no thanks' were words that either she didn't hear or just would not believe.

" I really am going to explode," I whispered to Fi, as Maria turned her back on us to grab another skewer. As I leant back, saying *"Grazie, basta, basta!"* (enough), Maria took advantage of the small space between my distended tummy and the plate, and loaded it up.

There was a Gary Rhodes style pyramid of sizzling meat that came almost to chin height. A slight sway forward and I could easily take a ' hands free ' bite. The children did their best to keep up too. Half way through they couldn't eat any more and so they went outside to play... we, however, had to plough on. Our hosts' generosity could not be faulted, it was only our capacity that was in serious doubt. Even if it has been proved to be a myth - I still like to think Romans had to have a *vomitorium* as an inter-course facility for just this kind of occasion - I wouldn't even need a feather to help me retch, the merest prod in the stomach would have done.

I left as much meat as I could around the tiny bones so that cleverly, every piece was fingered and bitten into. Somehow what remained on my plate, although looking like the day after a battle, appeared to have been respectfully tackled. Maria seemed pleased, so that was the main thing.

The others around the table looked pink and stuffed and we all shone with grease and perspiration; it looked as if we'd been firing-up a beam-engine. Suddenly, the children bustled in from the garden. Laurie was in a bit of state and Meri, Lucy and Ollie were behind him, all sobbing as they squeezed through the door.

"Oh dear, what's wrong ?" Fi asked.

Laurie shouted indignantly," It's awful... We've eaten the canaries!"

"Oh, no," Fi said... " Are you sure?"

"Yes," Meri added, her voice jerking between the tears, "they've ALL gone!"

I hadn't been totally sure what we'd been eating.

"No, no... it'sa alright, kids, it'sa alright", said Giovanni, now clearly upset too at the children's tears. He reassured us. It was all okay... the birds had simply gone to roost in the top of their cage, so couldn't be seen.

"Thank goodness."

The children, satisfied by the explanation, went back into the garden to check out the cages.

A wonderful thing honesty.

What we neglected to tell them, however, was that we had in fact eaten a flock of the unfortunate bunnies, instead - which at their tender age might have been just as upsetting. They never knew.

Hauling our full stomachs back along the path to the mill, through the fields of moonlit wheat, was one of the toughest walks I've ever had to make. We probably all still bear the stretch marks. (if there had been a pudding or even a wafer-thin mint, my memory has blanked it out). The only thing that lightened our load and our way home was the hundreds of fire-flies that glowed along the winding track, as if we were being guided home by the food fairies.

Another vignette from my sketchbook was our visit to Puglia, a taste of raw southern Italy. We stayed not far from the grand city of Lecce, known as the " Florence of the South ", the two thousand-year-old capital of the Salentine peninsula. In history, it was always closely linked with Greece and even now, a language called 'Griko' is still spoken in the region. It felt more exotic than Italy, with its columned buildings and palms - it was more like a colonial town in North Africa.

In Puglia one of the food specialities are the tiny pasta curls, known as Orecchiette. The name translates as 'little ears' and that's what they look like. It fascinated our kids and made them feel vaguely cannibalistic when eating them.

Another strange thing in the area are the *trulli* ; conical houses that look like stone fir-cones, but unlike the buildings of iron-aged of Cyprus, monks dwellings on Skellig Michael, wine makers huts of Rheinhessen in Germany, or even the pig-styes of St Fagans in Wales - these structures were not built with permanence in mind. The buildings are constructed of dry-stone walls, with no cement or mortar, and with a white collar and ball on top. They evolved, it's thought, as a form of taxation avoidance because they were classed as a type of building exempt of tax; when the tax-inspector turned up, a tug on the collar made the semi-permanent structure collapse. Slightly drastic, but no building equalled no tax! It evidently caused a whole region of tax evasion that eventually became a design statement too, and now it seems they are sought after as second homes for Brits and Germans escaping a taxing modern life.

We went on a day trip to the troglodyte town of Matera. It was the location for Mel Gibson's film *The Passion of the Christ*, which was appropriate not only because it looked like something from a Bible story, but also because it had been colonised by both Benedictine and Greek Orthodox monks in the 7th and 8th centuries. Some of the very first churches used for worship are on the slopes. The modern town sits on a shoulder of land above the old town which is thought to be 9,000 years old, making it one of the earliest human settlements, or as we were told the first 'city' in the World aparently, pipping even Damascus, Byblos and Sidon at the stone-aged post however if you don't believe that then it is certainly the earliest significant settlement in Italy.

At the edge of the modern town, the land drops away into what, at first, looks like an old quarry. It is a ravine known locally as *La Gravina*. After staring for a while into what appears to be a stone-age tip, it's possible to make out roofs, chimneys and then black holes for windows, all carved out of the 'tuff' rock. The large city is moulded out of the same colour stone as the cliffs and looks like a child's clay village. Once you get your eye in, a whole 'Flintstone' wonderland becomes visible. It's enormous, the dwellings cover the valley floor and spread up the cliff sides. Laid out before the observer is the metamorphosis from cave-dwelling into house. It's a history of architecture or the evolution of the human dwelling, from hole in the ground to building. Every structure has grown organically out of the caves. In its pre-Gaudi-like curves and contours, it resembles an uncontrolled plant-form or fungus more than a man-made city. It's hard to see the edges of each house, because they are the same sea-grey colour as the rock they emerge from. In some places, it's the path surrounding a structure that defines it, rather than its walls. There are walkways between the roughly hewn structures that jut out and wrap around bits of rock. Stairways surf up the cliffsides at unlikely angles and seem to defy perspective like an Escher drawing.

Apparently, the developer's main focus was on camouflage rather than what is usually the motivation for a new town; water. Over the millennia, it's evident that solving the civic water supply and drain-age problems has involved huge effort and man-power.

Having been considered a slum for many years, it has taken a long time for people take a second look at the dwellings and consider them suitable for twenty-first century housing. But now, some of the houses are being renovated for living in once again, which means there has been of continuous occupation since cave-man. I can imagine that when they are done-up, they must be the ultimate in 'trog-chic'.

Sometimes in a sketch pad, a line drawing can convey a subject more succinctly than a finished picture. Often, I will just add a few words to describe a particular colour, atmosphere or kind of light. The combination makes a visual note that is enough to jog the memory, should the drawing ever be worked up into a painting.

After a visit to Giotto's frescoes, which date back to 1304, in the Cappella degli Scrovegni in Padua, both our children were inspired to attempt to copy a part of it in their sketchbooks. I think it was a moment in both their childhoods that enabled them to see themselves as artists too. Giotto's work was certainly one of the major influences for Stanley Spencer. The naïve human forms are clearly taken a step further in some of Spencer's Cookham paintings and also at the Sandham Memorial wall paintings in Burghclere; a comparison of how they both painted angels shows the similarity in representation.

On an early television documentary about Spencer, when he is talking about his love of Giotto, in the idiom of the time, he says:

"What Ho! Giotto" - as a way of recognosing or respecting Giotto for the huge stylistic debt he owed him. The influence and interest in Giotto's painting and early Renaissance art in general, was probably more important to the Slade school's 'Coster Gang' of painters (Spencer, Paul Nash, Gertler, Nevinson and Carrington) than the ' modern ' art just being brought across the Channel by Roger Fry, before the First World War. It was fortuitous that Spencer had been introduced to Giotto and the writings of John Donne at the same time, by Gwen Darwin (later Raverat), or his journey in paint might have taken a very different path.

After a visit to the chapel in Padua, one colour stays in the mind; a vibrant but ageing blue; it syncopates off the walls and ceiling like Georgian discordant singing. The reason it is so pleasing, almost edible, is because through time, much of it has worn away what remains is a dusting and patching of colour on an earthy ground. The Angels float with dazzling golden halos on this background and time has turned the whole fresco into an element beyond even Giotto's intention. It's almost as if a greater hand has contributed in order to turn a mere painting into a celestial space.

The ageing process has, for once, worked in mankind's favour. I only wish we could resist the urge to restore too readily; am I the only one who thinks the time-ravaged Sistine Chapel was so much more venerable than the brand-new cleaned one? After all, what we are seeing is the restorer's vision instead of the Master's, aren't we? The addition of time should not be simply cleaned away, it is surely something the painting has earned, like respect?

There are always incredible moments, artistically speaking, on any journey around Italy. For instance, when we came across an unknown (to us) fresco cycle in Tolentino. It was like seeing the birth of religious passion for the first time and all the more amazing because we had simply wandered in off the street to grab some cloistered shade.

Or, when we visited the cells of a monastery in Florence where, luckily for the monks and for history, Fra Angelico happened to be the painter and decorator in residence and was called upon to 'brighten up' the walls.

One of the greatest artistic thrills for us came when we found the small Riccardi " Chapel of the Magi " in Florence, which had been built for the Medici family. Benozzo Gozzoli had been commissioned to paint a procession of nobles on horseback, on pilgrimage. The figures, in all their gold finery, are exquisite and have a reality rarely captured before, but it's the landscape behind them that really interested us. (The painting was so inspiring that over a two year period leading up to the millenium, we painted a wall-painting of friends and neighbours coming to an exhibition, on the East wall of our chapel (below) as a direct result.)

The background of the Medici Riccardi fresco is extraordinary; it transcends normality and meets fantasy somewhere in the middle. This is a depiction of the 'ideal' painted in a time when the perfect landscape could only be dreamt of. The countryside was a forbidding and dangerous place, and yet Gozzolli in his backgrounds has painted the landscape as a thing of sublime beauty. It is true artifice with its wonderfully elongated cypresses and umbrella pines and yet what he put down five hundred years ago is the visual metaphor for what we think of as the modern Italian landscape and it is certainly representative of the garden that we would like to have in Italy.

Talking of artifice, a trick of the mind... imagine walking through the same door that Leonardo did, when he was a boy. He no doubt would have just skipped through the small olive grove that led up to his house, perhaps picking up a silver-sided leaf with a worm on it, to study or to show his mother. Maybe he paused for just a moment to look over the wall at the town of Vinci, shimmering through a heat-haze in the valley, before he kicked open the door.

One of the magical things about being in Italy, is that things really have not changed a great deal since Leonardo'stime. It's still possible with only a small dose of imagination to get inside the insoles of many of the 'Great Artists' by physically walking in their footsteps. You can run your fingers around the rim of the pigment-grinding stone that Raphael used in his house in Urbino, or dip your feet in the same stream as Giotto did as a shepherd boy - and no doubt get similar chilblains.

The sultry heat, sounds of birds or insects and the smells are the same, the stone walls identical, and from Leonardo's house, the view down to Vinc hasn't changed significantly. It is possible to sketch scenery that may have remained almost unaltered for a few hundred years.

We were staying a walk away from Vinci with David, Jane and Howie, house-sitting for friends and looking after their animals. If Le Marche in summer is green and gold brocade, then Tuscany is ultramarine and faded denim. The colours are dictated by the climate and near Vinci, in late July, it's barbeque hot - all baked herbage and heat crazed roads. By mid-summer the sun has bleached-out the landscape like an old striped-canvas deckchair.Everywhere there are parallel lines seen through the blue haze; the neat vineyards, olive groves, gyrating *girasole* and rows of crackling crops. The old house that we were staying in overlooked a mixed grill of cooked fields that descended steeply down to Empoli. The view had the dull hue of an dusty mosaic that needs water tossed on it to make its colours live.

The solid stone house we were residing in for a few days sat four-square on a hill, with attitude, and was surrounded by various bits of ancient motor-cycles, rustic pergolas and huge ceramic olive oil-storage pots. It stood at the top of another tyre-shredding track and seemed to be sitting guard above the *orto*, willing to take on any stranger who dared venture up the hill. It was evident from the large garden that this was a place where the inhabitants relied on the food that was grown. (The owners have three little girls to support and share one lecturing job at Florence University).Salad crops,fruit and vegetables spilled over the ragged grass. There had been no attempt to tidy up between one harvest and the next. It looked like the food had simply been grabbed and dashed to the kitchen. There was a haphazard urgency in the planting; tomatoes hung in ruddy enormous bunches, bending their long-suffering supports, and multi-coloured squashes jested through the weeds, every imaginable edible vegetable and fruit could be glimpsed hiding in the undergrowth like forbidden fruit - a horticultural 'pick-and-mix'. It was aesthetically beautiful in its abundant productivity.

Especially charming, set amidst the jungle, was a small wooden ladder that lead one's eye up to an olive tree-house. There is something extra special about a child's house built in such an ancient tree. Some olive trees may have lived for four or five thousand years, is there another tree on the planet that represents life and continuity more? It symbolises the warmth and fecundity of the Mediterranean, and I think out of all the plants from these climes, it became the one plant that we wanted to grow some day. (Talking of ancient olives - we once visited the spot where Homer had his school on Ithaca, and were told by the archeaologists work-ing on the site - and have no reason to doubt the story although little is actually known of Homer - that he passed the very same olive trees that we had on his way to the sea, and even then they would have been old and twisted.) This olive tree-house was a place of romance for the young girls, somewherefor them to play out their Juliet and Rapunzel fantasies amongst the twinkling foliage and bitter fruit.

Like Venzano throughout the garden there were terracotta sculp-tures in unexpected places. Reclining Gauginesque figures watched from niches in the building. They also peeped out knowingly from behind wonky pergolas in the long grass. These sculptures added an unexpected element of cultural sophistication to the otherwise unkempt space. They imbued the garden with an understated bohemian intelligence, like Duncan Grant's battered but beautiful straw hat.

The girls' pets - a cat, rabbit and tortoise, were our charges; a simple matter of feeding all and occasionally ' airing ' the rabbit and tortoise from their large communal compound. All was fine for a couple of days and even the rabbit seemed to be happy to be hustled clumsily into his cage by David at the end of the day.

Then, in a well thought-out slight of paw, the rabbit set up a distraction; he unselfishly allowed the tortoise to make ' the long walk to freedom '. It made me wonder how long this break-out had been planned; the tortoise must have worked out his cover carefully over months. He took his chance while his owners were away. It was a leaf-to-leaf escape as cunning as gliding from Colditz. He had somehow made himself invisible from the instant he broke out of the compound. Our duties had not been that difficult and yet we had let the bungalow-on-legs get away... what would we tell its owners? The girls would be distraught. How was it possible for our ten guarding eyes to lose one of the slowest escapees on Earth? We literally did not leave a nearby leaf unturned... but he had gone. Howie (who's over sixty by the way, not six) spent the next three days gently prodding the undergrowth with a stick - in vain. He seemed content to occupy himself like one of the Famous Five in ' Hunt for the lost tortoise '. It took over his every waking hour and we all admired his thorough persistence. Each day he woke to think that this would be his lucky day and that he would prod a leaf and hear a hollow clank of wood on shell ... but it didn't happen.

The rest of us had long since given up hope, and chatted idly in the shade under the pergola, distracted by the heat and the prospect of a firework display and *festa* in Vinci on our last evening.

I had parked the car next to a restaurant in the centre of Vinci and the roads seemed unusually quiet. By the time we emerged, well fed, the town had transformed itself into a midnight market place with hundreds of small stalls selling *festa* produce associated with childlike-fun; toys and treats from shooting space-wheels to long florescent strings of liquorice. At least it was a bit of a distraction for Howie, who filled his pockets with lurid looking sweets and stopped mentioning the tortoise, at last. All was sparkling and luminous, including the parking ticket on our windscreen. Our car was now the lone vehicle in a town of pedestrian fun. I was going to have to do the ' drive-of-shame '. Driving up the main street with all its impressive line-up of street theatricals was going to be the equivalent of being hit by eggs whilst manacled in the stocks. There was no other way of getting out of town, I just had to brace myself and hope for the best. At what I consider to be a tortoise pace, I negotiated my way between the stalls in a slow zig-zag over guy ropes and in front of street acts, as they performed sets they'd been practising for a year. Too embarrassed to know what to do when I was forced to stop, I wound down the window and took the full-frontal abuse from an angry crowd. I obliterated the view of a particularly good band. I knew it was annoying, so I felt they deserved an explanation for my odd behaviour.

"*Sono Inglese*," I shouted, as a kind of excuse for my actions (but of course being Welsh really, I was mentally shifting the blame!).

Having suffered the jeers and boo's from driving through the pageant, I felt pretty shaky, so it was a relief to find a legal parking space at the top of town. I was just in time to join the others to watch one of the most spectacular firework displays I've ever seen. Somehow the enormous bursts of flashing flames (pure *pirotecno da Vinci*) were made all the more significant by the thought that Leonardo too would have no doubt stood on the very same spot to watch some kind of *festa* in his namesake town.

A few days later all five of us werewaiting for yet another firework display back in Ascoli Piceno. We were up on Jane and Howie's *altana* (roof terrace), watching the darkening southern sky, when something strange happened; out of all of us, David is pro-bably the least susceptible to the extraordinary and so I suppose him being with us was like having a 'control' to an experiment. Whatever we all saw that night was unexplainable or at least unidentifiable.

I was first to spot it; a hovering pinky/white disc, dipping and tilting just above the horizon. I said, " Wow, look at that... that's strange - it's like a giant frisbee surrounded by lights."

David said," It's probably something to do with the fireworks."

Then, about ten minutes later it reappeared, slightly closer. It seemed to be shimmering and hovering, and was now between us and the hills, below the horizon. Howie had at last seen it properly too, this time, "No, you're right Freddie, it's something unusual - the way it's propelling itself without a jet stream or anything... that's really weird!"

The third time it passed, after another short interval, it was closer still - almost overhead. Each time it passed it was travelling from right to left at about the same speed. Unbelievably, it passed for a fourth time and now we all had a close-encounter view; it seemed to be a classic UFO saucer or discus shape, surrounded by a miasma of pink smoke with small pin-pricks of light in a band around it's girth and there was also a darker inverted 'smile' shape on the rim. It seemed to be self-propelled and it's movements were quick and fluid. It also appeared to be if not spinning, then throb-bing slightly, like a jelly-fish.

This time even David had seen it properly and was sure it was something.

" Ohh... no, that is odd - I mean it's really not right - there's no engine noise, in fact it's completely sodding silent!" he exclaimed... and his voice seemed to squeak with an unusual show of emotion.

It was, of course one of those occasions when my camcorder battery had run out and all our cameras were somewhere downstairs. When I've told friends the story, they glaze over in disbelief and I know I've lost them.

I'm just telling it as it happened, I make no claims or judgements, so it has to remain a private experience between us five witnesses.

In the calmness of the morning, we all separately drew what

we had seen the night before and our drawings were identical, including the 'smile' shape. There is no explanation - we all just know what we saw. Howie looked for information on the internet and apparently there had been several reported sightings of UFO's in Le Marche, that night.

For Howie, at least, we hoped this new excitement would finally help him forget about the lost tortoise, as he'd been so upset about it. He has spent every night since on his *altana*, armed with all the photographic recording gear, but of course he'll never see the like again. When we texted him a few days later to tell him the good news that the tortoise had apparently come home in a thunder storm (they don't like the rain), he was quite disinterested... he'd moved on. He simply replied;

'What tortoise? All's quiet here on Altana ... signed, Captain Zog!'

Being a tonal painter I've always found that the dark shading provided by a soft pencil suits the way I work. Putting simple blocks of shade can record a scene as efficiently as a black and white photo. It's a quick method of capturing the atmosphere of a place, even showing what the weather was doing when pencil stroked paper.

On our many holidays, another way of recording a place that has been useful as a memory jogger, has been the camcorder, it has recorded our family history more personally than Pepys. It was a new toy and so was well used as our children were growing up.

One particular video I remember was on Meri's tenth birthday when we were staying at Peter and Richard's house. They had told us about a festival where people gathered together on top of a mountain near Cagli to celebrate the summer dawn after a full-mooned night. It sounded interesting and the kids were keen for an adventure, even if it meant a very early start. We set the alarm for three in the morning. After my years of early starts with the bakery, getting up early doesn't really worry me, but for the younger members of our family it was impossible. Suddenly the adventure had lost its appeal. We finally managed to load them both in the back of the car by bribing them with the thrill of seeing the dawn. They had plenty of time to grab extra sleep in the car as it took nearly two hours to drive on the winding track up to the top of the mountain. We kept climbing until we literally reached the end of road and we were on our own - there were no other cars. Had we got the wrong mountain? There was nobody about, not even people on foot, there was complete silence and the only light was coming from the bright full moon.

We could see that the real peak was still further up the mountain, so as we'd come this far we thought we might as well see the whole landscape down to Cagli laid out beneath us in the moonlight. As we approached the plateau top on foot, I could see a faint glow crowning its brow. Soon, it was possible to make out movement; small figures seemed to be silhouetted against the light, but so far away it was hard to make out what was going on. It was so strange to see activity on an otherwise silent mountain thousands of feet up on a dark morning. It was almost like coming across the landing sight of another extra-terrestrial visitor... Howie (Captain Zog) would have been in his element. As we got closer, other blanketed wanderers seemed to join us out of the darkness. Soon I could make out even more people plodding silently up the mountain, as if summoned to the summit like zombies.

Before long, we heard a mystical sound, wafting in waves through the darkness like incense. There is something transcendental about the sound of a plucked and sliding sitar and the bending beat of a pakhawaj drum - It was like reliving the first Beatles trip to India, or maybe their first 'trip' whilst there. That pumping rhythm - from Tuareg drums to Elvis' strums... or perhaps from Norwegian Dirges to Eminem's urges... it draws us in. This waving murmur of Indian music pulsed like a palpitation and pulled us towards it too. Even the children were wakened by its Eastern promise.

Just imagine how it felt... there we were up a mountain in Italy - in the dark... when suddenly we happened upon hoards of people, bright lights and continentally misplaced music. It was a multi-cultural shock to the system. In front of us were hundreds of people, listening intently to a challenging sitar virtuoso. To say it was like having indulged in a barrel load of 'shrooms' would be putting it mildly. I've done my fair share of festivals, I used to work at Reading Festival in the early Seventies, when it was still just a jazz and blues festival and when Glastonbury was still known as the Pilton Festival. We've even seen a Solstice dawn at Stonehenge, many years ago, however, this gathering was different from any I'd experienced before - it felt all-inclusive. Our children were comfy there too. Maybe because it was in Italy, or perhaps that it took place so early in the morning, but there was no aggressive or weird edge to the gathering, there were no really drunk, stoned or agitated people - it was a truly family event. Everyone seemed content to be there, just to enjoy the atmosphere, the moon and the music.

Short clips of the video show details; a large green grasshopper with smart black stripes, near someone's ear is about to enter the handbag they're using as a pillow... then there's a clip of the hypnotic thumb/palm motion of a drummer's hand... then some film of Laurie, wearing the hat Richard had given him, standing with hands on hips on the mountain's brink, a full-moon facing him like a life-challenge.

We listened to the music and spread ourselves out on the windblown grass. The tempo of the drumming seemed to gather pace as we waited for the sunrise. Anticipation was building as the vague glow turned into incandescence - soon, the sun's rays took to the air creating a feeling of wild exultation. Several people stood worshipping it, arms held high like high priests at a virginal sacrifice. Great fanning projections of light cut into the sky behind the edge of the mountain as dawn knifed through the air. Even before its appearance, there was a promise of heat. We were all being warmed by geometric and thermal degrees as the sun shafted acute angles through the long grass. People were being branded in segments from brow to breast. In symmetry, the Sun rose on one side of the mountain as the Moon descended on the other. For just an instant, there was feeling of perfect Libran balance and oneness;

a moment that's said to be like meeting an ' Angel from Heaven'. This ultimate moment of harmony could be seen as the best present for a tenth birthday, despite the early rise.

The changing of the guard from Moon to Sun was far quicker than at Lenin's tomb (which we saw in the 1980's), or at Buckingham Palace, it was all over in a couple of minutes. A peak had come and gone, the boil had been burst, the climax had been reached. Now without purpose, the momentarily animated army of photovoltaic freaks dis-persed quite quickly and silently.They were, however, elated rather than deflated, as though they had seen what they needed to see, and so were quite happy to retire to their dwellings until the next time. The party up the mountain was over and we needed breakfast... and anyway, there were some presents to unwrap.

The video recording quickly jumps down the mountain and back to the bedroom, where Meri has just started to unwrap her birthday presents. Unfortunately, unlike the camera, Meri has had to suffer another two hours descending the sickening hairpin bends; the soundtrack of the film just picks up the sound of her retching in the bathroom as I poignantly zoom in on the abandoned unwrapped presents on her bed...

Fiona sketches in a different way from me. Her drawings are done with a fine-leaded pencil and they are detailed studies of botanical accuracy. The pages of her sketch books are more like the journal of a plant hunter on one of Cook's voyages (I'm sure Joseph Banks might have apprenticed her, had women been allowed on the *Endeavour*) and she has recently painted a globe of a visionary journey which seems appropriate. Individual specimens are dissected on the page with parts labelled, as though they are to be used for a scientific experiment. This passion for plants in particular, and nature in gen- eral, turns any walk into a botanical expedition, so when Joy and Nigel, friends who share the interest (fellow 'plant-heads'!) came to stay with us in the spring, I knew that walking down the mountain opposite the house was going to take hours. I decided my time could be better spent cutting grass so volunteered to take them up the mountain by car and drop them off. I took them to the top of Monte Sant'Angelo where there is a small church with an oversized iron-cross and a viewing point (the very cross that caught the sun on my first visit to the house). The panorama from the summit is hard to take in; there is the Adriatic on one side and the Apennines on the other and in between is a wrinkled newspaper of folded hills. It's exactly as though someone has crumpled the landscape into a ball by mistake and then tried to flatten it out again before anyone notices, leaving a complexity of guilty creases. On a clear day, it's possible to see the distant lump of city statedom that is San Marino, about seventy miles to the North.

The plan was that I would pick them up in two hours at the bottom of the mountain, which at normal walking speed takes about an hour to descend, but the extra time would allow them to study the flowers on the way.

On my way back down, I stopped where a derelict cottage overlooks Arcevia and the bright turquoise Adriatic. It really is a paradise spot, one of the most perfect places I can think of…and yet is also the saddest. For it was on this site that the Nazis, with a cruelty beyond efficiency, shot dead 63 people. Not only did they line up and shoot some partisans but also the entire Mazzarini family who lived in the cottage and had been suspected of nothing more than feeding the partisans. The Nazis were infamous for their massacres, (we've been to the spot on the cliffs in Kefalonia where they 'disposed' of nearly 5,000 Italian soldiers,) but despite the difference in numbers this seems just as horrific. To kill women, old people and young children in such a quiet and sublimely beautiful place makes the violation seem all the more brutal.

I once asked Ido how he felt about the massacre, as he knew the people that were killed and who are buried in the local cemetery. He simply shrugged his shoulders, his gnarled palms facing skywards like a mannerist painting and said, in the tone of a man who has seen life :

"Well," … he paused… "all Nationalities did bad things in

the War." He seemed to have been able to forgive - I'm not so sure I could have been so magnanimous.

We've seen the rare Edelweiss flower on the top of the mountain and it seems to symbolise a new 'Sound of Music' harmony in the European family of nations. If flowers are your passion, as Fi will tell you, then the walk down the mountain is equivalent to a 'twitcher' sprouting wings. There are so many rare plants just along the roadside that there is barely any need to venture off the track to feel fulfilled. Every few seconds entails a bent-double study; it's a back-breaking and a time-consuming occupation... I had already been phoned to delay the pick-up by another hour.

Fi finds it rewarding knowing the names of plants, it's like a primal need to engage in the 'naming of names'. These are just some of the flowers they spotted; it's almost as exciting just saying their names as seeing the flowers; the spider orchid and its cousin the 'Italian' spider orchid, the lady orchid, Provence orchid, early purple orchid, the man orchid and the Italian man orchid, pyramid orchid, fragrant orchid and the violet birds-nest orchid. All these rare wonders poking through cerise carpets of wild cyclamen and anemone hortensis, white star of Bethlehem, red vetchling and golden dyers greenwood. An artist's palette of colour, laid out amongst the wooded slopes above Arcevia.

Joy was also busy bending over to collect oak apple galls for dyeing her wool. The strange dipping movements of the threesome aroused the curiosity of an old man driving by. He kept turning around and passing them again and again very slowly, just staring. At first, they thought he was some kind of pervert but then realised that he was probably worried that they might have discovered a treasured truffle area. They were totally engrossed in the natural world, even taking a few minutes to poke a stick at a pile of fresh wild-boar crap. I hate to be so mundane, but it was all eating into the time we were supposed to be using to catch the last of the shops in Arcevia that evening... I decided I had better try to pick them up, pretty sure that as five hours had now passed, they must be nearing the bottom of the mountain.

I started driving up the mountain to meet them but by the time I was nearly half way up I presumed I must have already passed them somewhere - maybe they had been in a field as I'd driven by. Just as I was turning to go back down, around the corner they ambled. They looked tired, but glowed with satisfaction. It had been one of the best walks of Fiona's life, she said never before had she seen so many orchids, they'd counted thirteen different types in all - a positive orgy of orchids - a kind of botanist's bacchanalia.

I've always meant to take time out to sketch on the journey to Italy. We pass through more than twelve hundred miles of ever-changing European landscape. But somehow, on the drive my attention is always elsewhere. I find it hard to concentrate on small detail when there is such a vast distance to cover and I just need to get on with it. Normally it takes two full days with an overnight stop near the French / Italian border.

Every time we drive past Bethune, Arras, Vimy Ridge and Lille in Northern France, it reminds me of my grandfather and the few First World War stories I gleaned from him whilst I was writing a thesis on Wilfred Owen, the war poet. My grandfather's story was told, almost exactly, in the novel *Birdsong* by Sebastian Faulks (before that book, explaining to people that my grandfather spent much of the war underground was not believed). He, too, was in the Royal Engineers and had to tunnel under no-man's land, trying to blow up the German front line by placing massive amounts of explosives under the enemy's lines. He told me that sometimes, they would hear the Germans tunnelling along-side them, going in the other direction doing the same as they were. Occasionally, the opposing miner's tunnels would meet and there would be hand to hand fighting underground.

Although he went right through the war, and was badly wounded at Vimy Ridge, he still considered himself fortunate to be with the

Royal Engineers, especially compared to the infantry, I remember him saying how moving it was seeing a gallant Scottish regiment being piped and drummed up to the front during the Battle of the Somme and how so few of them made the return journey. We all know the appalling casualty figures for that seemingly useless war, but the other day it was really brought home to me; when broken down to a daily death-toll for combatants from all sides, the figure is five thousand human beings, every day from 1914 to 1918, or more graphically, that's like wiping out a full house at the Albert Hall every single day for four years.

He also told me how he watched the dog-fights over Arras (by 1917 the life expectancy for a pilot was only seven days). No doubt he would have seen the British fighter ace Albert Ball who was second only to ' the Red Baron ' in his number of successful missions. Finally, he too was shot down near Arras, just one of the 14,000 airmen killed in the war. He received the VC posthumously, aged only twenty .

Like so many others, my grandfather's war ended with the flu (Spanish influenza killed over forty thousand service men at the end of the war). Taken ill at the front, he was told he'd have to walk with full kit to the nearest dressing station, over twelve miles away. In his condition, the 'walk' was almost enough to finish him off. He described crawling on all fours along muddy ditches at the side of the road, willing himself on although all his strength had gone. He eventually made it and collapsed in a hospital bed, where he was out cold for over a week. The temporary hospital was actually an old chateau and when he finally felt able to get up and go for a little walk in the grounds, he was surprised to see several large marquees in the garden, it was surreal. Still feeling slightly delirious, he assumed some kind of party was going on. But when he pulled open the canvas, to his horror the marquee was stacked from floor to ceiling with corpses - victims of the terrible flu, waiting to be buried.

It's hard not to remember Europe's war-veined history when driving through France - the road signs read like a compendium of battles; Crecy, Agincourt (if we go via Germany), Somme, Verdun etc.

Last summer, we uncovered a strange link with a distant war when we were wandering around Urbino after lunch with Fiona's parents, Fi's mum dropped a piece of family history into the conversation like a casually lobbed chunk of pasta. She said; " When I was four, we moved house and my mother inherited a tenant whom she agreed to look after for the rest of his days. He was a frail old man who had lived in the woods outside a small village in the Welsh Valleys, for as long as anyone could remember. He was still wearing the ragged remains of his old army uniform. He was a deserter from the War.."

" What the First World War, like the deserter in ' Cider with Rosie' ?" Fi asked.

"Oh No, the American Civil War. I remember him... he still wore a tattered blue uniform ," Binny replied.

We all stopped, in utter amazement. Fi's mum went on " He called himself Charlie Black but his real name was George Brown, we found out after he died. He had somehow escaped from America during the Civil war when he was about sixteen or so, and ended up in Wales. He'd been too afraid to ever go back."

We quickly tried to work out the maths, if he'd been twenty, or younger in the mid 1860s he could have been in his late eighties or early nineties when Binny was a young girl. An incredible passing of a verbal history ' baton ' in a relay of just two memories, spanning a hundred and fifty years.

It was one of those moments that opened up the possibility of straddling centuries with a very personal experience, like looking at the board in a Norman church that has a list of all past vicars - sometimes as few as twenty names span the centuries back to its construction.

Sometimes it can take one right back to ' Norman the Conqueror ' himself!

If the battlefields of France, are just too much to take, there is always the alternative route. Although slightly further we have driven through Germany and Austria into Italy just for a change. The scenery through the Tyrol is worth the extra effort. It always induces a titter when we drive past the signpost to Wank mountain on the Austrian border.

I have a puerile fantasy of being at the barbers' having a haircut for the trip. The barber making small talk would ask:

"Doing anything nice for your holidays, sir"

To which I could reply:

"Not really… I'm just going to Wank for a fortnight!"

FUN AND SUN

Sig. Tortaloni has been pivotal in our smooth transition to life in Italy. Although it is quite tricky for us to understand what he's saying... Not only does he have a strong local accent, he also tends to talk with a fag in one corner of his mouth and gum in the other.

He is evidently much respected in the locality. His family owned a vineyard near our house, so he is rooted in the geography of the landscape around us. We feel fortunate that he became our *geometra* by chance, as Jeff and Alessia just happened upon him when looking for a *geometra* in our area.

His official work for us has been concerned with the renovation of the house. He has organised the builders from the quote through to the design bit and on to the completed project, taking only a small percentage for each job. One thing we have found in Italy is that when the builder submits a quote for a job, instead of whacking on hidden, unexpected extras, they do the opposite; every time so far, the actual bill has come in under the sum quoted, which always makes you feel you've done better than expected. Also we've been really impressed that every job we've had done has been comp-leted faster than originally promised - all much better for builder / client relations. Of course, it's in the builders interest to keep 'in' with the *geometra* because that's where his future employment lies. The builder's performance is being constantly overseen by the geometra and that inbuilt quality control satisfies all parties.

    I was amazed too that when we had a bathroom tiled (we had to get rid of the rather rude ' fanny tiles '), we were charged for so many boxes of tiles and the unused ones were left neatly in boxes in the *cantina*. When I tried to give away some left-over roofing felt and the old satellite dish to the builder, he took a great deal of reassuring that it would be fine. Sig. Tortaloni seems to have taken on the job as our ' minder '. I discovered early on that it was quite nice to be treated as the idiot foreigner. If you don't speak the language too well or just look a bit lost, people tend to look after you... Italy is a matriarchal culture, so they naturally want to mother you.

    Actually, I didn't have to pretend that I was stupid with him, because I understood so little of what he was saying, he was all too used to my blank expression. Finding out that we still had to go all the way to the Fabriano police station to register as foreign aliens every few months seemed to make him really cross. He grabbed hold of me in his office and dragged me up Corso Mazzini (almost by my ear). We picked up some kind of *francobolli*, (stamps) from the newsagents', on our way. Then we went to the civic building. He shoved me in front of a young police-woman and insisted that we be made 'residents' immediately. She duly obliged!

    If ever there is a problem, we know he's there, on our side and eager to help - like with the flies, for instance. So it was to him we turned when our house was struck by lightning.

    It was a cool and stormy evening in July, so Meri, Fi and I were eating indoors (almost unknown in summer). There are sometimes very dramatic thunderstorms up on our hill and this one was particularly close, the lightning and the thunder-claps were happening at the same time - those are the ones you've always been warned to be wary of, we now know for good reason. The windows were rattling and the house felt as though it was trembling under the storm's strafing. We were really glad to be in the safety of our cosy home. Fiona was cooking and she had just put a ladle on the work surface, when suddenly the whole storm entered the house; first there was an explosion and an ear-syringing blast, followed by a great ball of rolling white light. It's hard to describe the light because it was beyond the spectrum - it was so white it was almost black if that makes any sense. Everything appeared in negative and the wrong way round; a black and white picture of the window frame was imprinted on the back of my eyeballs for the duration.

The fiery ball - it was more of an impression of a ball than a real shape - blasted from one corner of the sitting room to the other (in less than a hundred micro-seconds,I learnt later). My first thought was that the cooker had exploded, because of a power surge, and not that it was lightning - it all happened so quickly but it took quite a few minutes to recover and to check that we were all still in one piece. The negative window frame picture in my head had now been replaced by bursting reddish bubbles.

I knew the electricity had gone... we were in darkness. The fuse box often trips , so that was normal. I went to switch it back on but the fuse box had been blown apart. It was still attached to the wall, but now had ominous bits hanging from it.

The thunderbolt made a direct hit. It had struck (and dented) the revolving silver cowl on the chimney stack and then had shot down the lightening conductor or the wiring... it had then literally pole-axed the fuse-box, deconstructing it.

We checked around the room for any other damage, nothing was obvious... but several minutes later when Fi tried to pick up the metal ladle on the work top, it was still too hot to touch! Later on, we also discovered that something inside the microwave oven had blown - probably because it had been plugged in, even though it wasn't on. It never worked again. Fortunately, we run a very low-tech house, or else other things like computers or televisions would have been destroyed too.

We hadn't got a clue who to go to for help after such a bizarre occurrence, after all who's responsible for thunderbolts? Our first thought to get help and advice was to go and see Sig. Tortaloni in Arcevia. We felt he would know how to put things straight. Sure enough, before we'd finished telling him the story, he was already on the phone to ENEL (the Italian electricity people). More impressive even than that - as we arrived back at the house (a ten minute drive from town)… an ENEL electrician got out of his van behind us on the track with a fuse box under his arm. It was fixed gratis because it had been damaged by an ' act of God, ' so there was our answer to the responsibility question too.

One of our biggest projects in the garden could have done with divine help too. We needed to move the Earth itself. What we wanted was to remove a bank of earth near the house and create a gentle slope. Then, we intended to plant grass-seed on it, making a continuous lawn that flowed smoothly around the house. Also, we wanted to dig away a small bit of the bank at the front of the house to enlarge the parking area. The removed earth was to be dumped over the edge of the land, on top of the old concrete kennel. I used a tangle of chicken wire, attached to the kennel, to contain the soil on the slope, like a gabion. This would extend the garden in a semi-circle, making a new area to jut out into the view, on which we could put a table and chairs to enjoy the scenery. We had already started to make a garden in a small way - there was of course the olive tree, symbol of ' the dream ' in the middle of the rough lawn and there were even the first signs of flower borders along the edges. We thought the addition of this little seating area would be just the thing to finish it all off.

Sig. Tortaloni said that he would arrange the hire of a mini-digger for the following day.

We awoke early to the sound of heavy-metal on tarmac coming from the other side of the valley. I spotted the gigantic yellow earth-mover moving over the earth... towards us.

"Bloody Hell," I said, "I hope that isn't our digger?"

" No," replied Fiona, confidently," that must be a farmer. Ours is going to be a mini-digger - it'll probably be delivered on the back of a truck."

The caterpillar tracks of the huge machine clanked and scraped through the silence like a division of Panzer tanks. The realisation that it was ' ours ' dawned on us slowly as it made its way to San Giovanni. It definitely didn't seem to be turning off to anybody else's place.

It took twenty anticipatory minutes for the monster to make its way past the cemetery, through the peace of the village and down our track. We heard it the whole way getting gradually louder. It was all too much for us to face. So as it inched passed the house we hid upstairs - we couldn't deal with the situation. We took turns to peep down at the great yellow machine from the bathroom window. The water in the lavatory bowl trembled as it almost scraped the side of the house. The maxi-digger was making a mini-earthquake. It was no good, we had to confront it. We emerged as it came to halt in the garden. It was stationary now but wheezing like an asthmatic walrus. Sig. Tortaloni had followed behind in his car. We explained that we felt that the huge JCB was a bit over the top for the job in hand - It was only a little bit of help with the garden that we needed.

Sig. Tortaloni just shrugged his shoulders and assured us it would be fine. He added with some kind of builder's logic that although: " it cost twice the price, the job would be done in half the time!" Sandro, the driver, complete with smart leather driving gloves and glinting blue eyes, looked keen to start the day of destruction. The impressive dragon clawed, scraped, gouged and scooped - it coughed out acrid mustard coloured fumes as it took greedy bites out of the bank. Then it lurched backwards in loops, reversing around the olive tree to dollop the spoil in great piles at the edge of the land.

The first few minutes of this gardening power were quite thrilling, the sheer brutish force was nerve tingling, every venting of its throaty roar vibrated through my chest.One could transform any landscape with one of these toys. It was even better than a strimmer as the ultimate garden 'must-have', or so I thought.

But every journey back and forth (and there were many) churned up any semblance of a lawn that we had created. An hour into the work and I had resigned myself to the fact that we would have to start again from scratch, I just couldn't even watch anymore. The thrill had gone.

The harsh reality was that our neat little garden had disappeared. What we had now was a scene from Ypres circa 1916. All we needed to complete the devastation was the smell of gas... I spoke too soon.

Sandro couldn't hit a gas main because we didn't have one. However, as luck would have it, he managed to locate the mains water pipe underground instead. The torrent of water was pretty impressive, our water pressure being unusually high. It gushed, pushed and squirted in equal amounts, making fleeting rainbows through its many fluted columns. An unexpected fountain or water feature always adds an element of pneumatic and kinetic surprise to a garden. And yes, we were truly taken aback by this powerful and unexpected display. Within minutes it filled all the ruts, tracks and trenches to the brim. In no time, the excess water flooded what was left of the old garden that was, as yet, untouched by the digger. We now had a kind of impromptu Alhambra (an interesting garden, true - but not what we were after here). Sandro had obviously performed this trick before - he was quite focussed and cool as he considered the problem. He calmly watched the torrent whilst pulling his gloves off, finger by finger. Then, taking his time, he looked around for the nearest dry place above the floodplain to lay out his precious driving gloves. There seemed no real urgency in his movements, but meanwhile I was re-evaluating the increasing damage... second by second. Nice to be so calm when it's not your problem, I thought.

He knew exactly what various tools would be needed to

repair the pipe and he barked orders like a surgeon: " scalpel... loppers...hammer... (and swabs!)". What the garden really needed now was a good post-operative swabbing. In only ten or so minutes, he had pruned a branch of wood from a fig tree and painstakingly whittled the stick with the knife into a Pinocchio-nose like plug shape... in fact he did the whole thing twice, as the first plug was just a fraction too small... what a craftsman I thought. Then he hammered it into the end of the water pipe to stop the flow.

The small audience of villagers who seemed to have arrived with the water, applauded as the flow was stemmed. It was such a relief when the flood stopped that even I clapped.

By the end of that traumatic day, we tried to see what we had learned or even gained from the experience; yes, we had created an area for a table. Yes, we had expanded the parking area and yes, we had met some of the village. They came down to see what was going on and were able to return home having had a good laugh at the new water garden we had made.

However, a little tip I feel I should pass on for anyone about to move earth around their garden... just remember to keep the top soil to one side. Ours had been dumped in the first loads over the edge and was now buried twenty feet under our new seating area.

What we had been left with was useless subsoil to make our new Mediterranean garden out of. The earth was so clayish now that it actually shone like porcelain in the moonlight that night and for many months to come.

With every visit, the house grew more homely. It started to fit us and we, it. Our visits took on another level of familiarity. It was becoming like a friend and no longer just a place of decorative projects. At last, we were actually able to do our own work, painting and drawing. Even though there was still plenty to do to the house, we and it, seemed to have accepted that we were here for the long term and that there was no rush. Relaxation was now at last, on a par with renovation. Just walking around the boundary, looking at the view in the warmth was like a massage of the senses. At last I could pick out a solitary farm from the vastness and just enjoy it. A whole afternoon could slip by just watching as the shepherd moved his flock to new pastures; it was possible to see the whole picture by studying the detail. We didn't need to be looking constantly at the view as though it was going to be taken away. Our confidence grew that it was going to be there even if we had to spend the day indoors. I think this significant change in outlook was the turning point - the stage when you cease to be on holiday and you start actually living in another place. We now found our-selves doing things like keeping our shutters shut to keep the summer sun out in an authentically Italian manner (something we would never have thought would happen).

There was still so much to do, but we were succumbing to a more local way of ' being '; the state of mind that comes with the Mediterranean climate. It's a kind of drug hanging in the hot air like the odour of ripe figs that stops you caring so much about the things in life that don't matter. It is possible to adopt another culture through the skin; the hot air opens the pores and then it's absorbed like aromatherapy.

We were undergoing a gradual evolution towards a slower pace of living. Everyday seemed to be a half-day holiday, like Dewi Sant's day in Brecon (March 1st), with a siesta in the middle. It was just like having a 'two-for' day, every day. Of course, there was still a great deal of work to be done but our attitude had definitely changed. The house as I have explained was covered in a grey and very unattractive concrete render and each window had two brown, stained shutters. It was an unbelievably drab exterior and we knew that it had to be painted.

Fi started on the windows and shutters. Fortunately, they are designed to slide easily off their hinges, so at least they could be propped against something in the garden and painted outside, in the dappled shade. I'm very impressed with the overall design of the windows; not only are they simple to slip off their hinges, the actual pane of glass slides into the top of the window frame.

It's tightly wedged between two slats of wood in the frame, so there's no need for putty and one can remove it easily for painting. There were 24 shutters, 24 window frames and two doors, all to be painted turquoise-green. It took a whole summer to get the job slowly and meticulously done. The house looked better and more cared for, as green slowly replaced shabby brown, all around the building.

I had given a great deal of thought to painting the outside of the house on my own. I have done big painting jobs before; every year I repaint the studio walls for our exhibition (being an old chapel the ceiling is over thirty feet high). However, I did find the idea of painting a whole tall house a bit daunting. Also it would be dangerous without proper scaffolding, so we came to the conclusion that we should have it done professionally.

We already had the colour in our minds, from that very first day, when we saw the apricot house in Fabriano. I mixed up our 'ideal' colour from memory, in oil paints on paper at home in the studio. It was a glowing pinky/orangey/apricoty colour, with a great deal of light in it (I wanted to try to achieve the luminosity of a cloud at sunset, if possible). Often, house colours can be very flat and opaque. These days, it is possible to have the colour you want mixed exactly, by computer. The house's masonry was to be the same tone as the shutters, so that they would play off each other, just like the Fabriano house. So I made colour swatches of the same colour but of three varying tones (brighter to paler), of both the pink colour for the walls and the turquoise/green for the shutters.

We were heading towards spring, and in a few weeks we would be able to show sig.Tortaloni and see which of the three he thought would be acceptable to the local *comune* (like a local council in England but possibly more powerful). On our way through Arcevia to see sig.Tortaloni and then the planning office, to get our colours approved, we passed a house with almost the same colour as we wanted. I took a photo of it to show, as evidence, if needed, that our colour was already being used in the area. We felt pretty confident that at last we would be able to give the house a face-lift.

I took out the pieces of water-colour paper with the coloured squares and laid them side by side on sig.Tortaloni's desk, under his nose ...

"No," he said , hardly even looking at them.

"What do you mean?" I said.

He drew up his shoulders in a slow, dismissive shrug. Without looking at us, he pulled out his own colour swatch from the desk drawer. He spread the fan of colours out from one corner on a pivoting rivet with the slickness of a cardsharp:

" *Questa, non è possibile,* " he said, pointing at our lovely apricot pink. Then he waggled his finger negatively in the air and let it fall like a divining rod, with force, onto his preferred colours. This was what we really wanted; firstly, a hideous brown, then a shite coloured ochre, followed by an equally unthrilling mouldy olive green. At last, he looked up at us, cigarette dangling from his mouth with an inch of ash teetering over his precious colour fan. I diplomatically nudged his spectrum of sludge out of the way, easing my camera under his nose.

" Look, we've just seen this house in Arcevia, ten minutes ago. So, I think we'll at least give it a try with the *comune*."

He peered at the photo screen for a few seconds through a cloud of smoke. Then he leered up at us, grunted, stubbed out his cigarette and rose to his feet without a word. He held the door open for us, a sign that now we should go to the *comune* planning office. He was utterly convinced that we had no chance with our colour, but if we wanted to be stubborn, then he was happy to let the officials put us in our place.

It felt exactly like waiting next to the headmaster's study, all three of us in a line outside the planners office, standing in silence. The tension was tangible and the corridor was stuffy - was the heating on full? The camera strap kept slipping off my clammy shoulder and I could feel the swatches of water-colour paper deck-ling along their edges. We could hear the planning official's voice rise and fall in a lengthy altercation. Through the straw-glass door I could just make out a gesturing arm as the animated conversation went on and on. Eventually, the door opened and a small woman emerged, close to tears. She tried to hide her eyes with a wad of papers as she passed by.

Without a pause we were called in; *"Avanti,"* bellowed the voice, in a deep basso profundo. This man was ' King ' of all he surveyed and as chief surveyor, our colourful future lay in his hands. He stood behind his large desk. He was tall, standing with legs astride, like 'the Jolly Green Giant' (but he wasn't green and didn't appear to be very jolly either...) his arms were folded, Il Duce style.

I hardly dared to broach the subject of our choice of paint maybe we could just settle for white? He didn't look the sort to like colour at all let alone our vibrant colour. He remained standing and motionless, staring into the distance. Coyly, I laid the most daring of the colour tones on the table in front of him first, then, I thought, we could compromise with the paler alternatives. I felt like a carpet-weaver laying a magic carpet at a Sultan's feet for his fickle approval. I was wincing within, waiting for the inevitable sword to fall.

I started to ask if he thought this colour would be suitable in San Giovanni. I could see sig.Tortaloni out of the corner of my eye; there was a " now you'll have to use dung brown " smirk on his face.

I was already groping blindly for camera back-up.

The planning officer glanced down casually, looked briefly at our colour choice, then flicked the paper as though he was flicking a fly off the table and without a second thought, said:

" Si, ... arrivederci." and gestured towards the door.

Was that it? ... really, that was it?... we'd won our approval, just like that.

Sig.Tortaloni said, in justification, that the *comune* were obviously having a mad phase. They were choosing bright colours this year - a passing trend, and if we wanted his advice, we couldn't go wrong with vomit green.

No thanks.

We assumed, it only being April, we could employ painters immediately and have a pretty painted house by the summer. Apparently not. We would have to wait - sig. Tortaloni explained that any ' good ' decorators would be booked up for months in advance. They didn't work on outside paint jobs during the summer because the paint dried too quickly on the brush.

We would just have to be patient and wait until November... eight whole months away. There was nothing we could do. Actually, in Britain, I think we have rather lost the ability to wait for things, we tend to just have a tantrum or find someone else for the job; if one shouts loudly enough or pays over the top, anything can be done. This rather spoilt attitude doesn't seem to work in Italy and actually, to wait a while for something certainly makes one appreciate it more, especially if it really turns out to be 'the best'.

We've noticed that as yet, Italians are not driven by money in the same way as the British are. Quality of life, rather than size of pay-packet still reigns supreme. In the Marche certainly, the income is just a means of having enough money to carry on with an enjoyable lifestyle. A lot of people choose to work half a day or part of the week; this allows them time for the really important things in life, like long lunches at the beach or in the garden, with friends or family - afternoons of cycling, swimming or just chilling.

They tend to prefer to rent an apartment rather than be saddled with a mortgage for life. The even luckier ones just move in with their *nonna*, so have no rent or mortgage to pay… and all meals cooked!

A huge amount of time is spent by Italians indulging in pleasurable pursuits that also supplement the income. It is a matter of pride as well as prudence to be as self-sufficient as possible, whether it's growing food or hunting, fishing, brewing, bottling, salting, baking, drying or even just generally foraging in woods, fields or hedgerows. They take pride in retaining the small-holding mentality whether they live in an apartment in town, or in a modern house on the outskirts or a village.

Often, in the basement of a new apartment block, there is a communal *cantina* for the storage of wild foods. It's a place where the hunting males can bring home the bacon, quite literally, and hang, cure or roast it. These cellars are reminiscent of hunting lodges, bedecked with trophies from hunting, and a place to hang the hams and store jars of fruit or veg and other preserves from the field or allotment. Also, it's somewhere for the whole apartment block to get together for feasts and festas.

Particularly if they live and work in the city, many Italians still seem to retain that urge to be earthed, even if they aren't drawn to return to their country roots completely. They need to feel the dirt between their fingers and the cold air of a winter morning on their faces as they go hunting.

They don't seem to live to work; they work to live, and they live a good life. Maybe that's why Italy, and apparently Le Marche (even though they are the biggest meat-eaters in Italy), is the place to be if you want to live to a well-ripened old age.

We first saw the house in its new livery from a distance (it was now possible to see it from a very great distance), and WOW was it bright! As we came down the track, even before rounding the bend, we could sense that something luminous was a'coming by the glow on the Acacia tree-trunks. The full strength of the colour hit us as we got out of the car (the tinted windscreen had taken the full stridency away). We stood in silence, trying to take in this alien life form that seemed to have fallen from outer space and was still glowing after re-entry.

We were not disappointed however, it was exactly like the colour I had mixed back home, just scaled up a thousand-fold. Even in the weak wintry sun, sun-glasses were essential when walking around the outside of the house. The painters had done a really thorough job, and they had been worth waiting for; sig.Tortaloni had been right. They had surrounded the whole place in scaffolding and masked everything like windows, door and even the paths around the base of the house. The whole job had been done with brushes and rollers it was a thick, impenetrable coat of luminosity (just like a glowing cloud at sunset, in fact). Within a few moments, we had recovered from the shock and genuinely, if cautiously, loved it. Talk about putting life into the old house. The painters reassured us that within a year or so the house would mellow into a beautiful earthy colour like the tiles on the roof....

The transformation of the house from drab grey to bright orange seemed to make the actual house proud of itself too. It no longer skulked behind the bushes - suddenly, it was out there ' strutting its stuff ' in a very Italian way. It had even suddenly achieved local fame (or notoriety); we were walking around the hill town of Barbara, which is probably ten kilometres from our house, as the crow flies, and got chatting to a local. When we told him where we lived he immediately said ; " *Aah, ca' rosa, si, I know your house, certo!*"

"Oh dear, it is a bit bright, isn't it ," said Fi, embarrassed .

"No, no it will age like a good wine, or a beautiful woman," he said...

I thought, "Don't men talk a load of shite…?"

Not only were we recovering from the house colour but also the bit of good news that we had just heard from home; as we had been approaching the house in the car, having just spotted the colour through the trees, our mobile rang. With one eye on the bright orange, and one ear concentrating on the phone, Fiona answered, whilst I stopped the car....

"Hi Mum, Laurie here, I've just had some great news… Damien Hirst has bought three of my paintings, and he is going put one of them in the Serpentine show in London, his personal collection!"

We seem to always be in Italy when Laurie or Meri give us this kind of exciting news. That is one of the problems of being out of the country quite often, it does impede or delay celebrations.

Laurie's painting went into Hirst's ' Murderme' exhibition in the Serpentine Gallery. The chosen painting was titled ' Spot the Dogging ' and depicted an attractive woodland scene, in naive style, with rude things going on in the corners. My mother proudly and innocently showed a reproduction of the painting from the newspaper to her hairdresser,

"Oh, Eira," the hairdresser said, " you don't know what 'dogging' is, do you dear…?"

"Yes, I do," said my mother, pointing at the picture; " look, there's a dog in it… there!"

Laurie and Meri were with us to help with one of the most important artistic jobs; turning our old potting shed into a studio. The concrete shed, that former residence of the bunch of hornets, was crammed full of old rubbish. David and Val had been there at the start of the clearing, and with four of us helping, the job I had dreaded only took a day. Smelly bags of animal feed, pots, bottles, old broken tools, shoes and bits of clothing were taken, journey after journey, in the car to the large recycling bins in town. The shed, about 8' by 10' was emptied of shelves and contents until it was a bare concrete shell. In scale, it was about the size of Dylan Thomas' writing shed at Laugharne in Wales. His shed overlooked an inspiring view of an estuary and the walls were covered with postcards and photos of friends. We very much hoped that our little potting shed could turn out to have a similar feel...

(I've always felt an empathy with Dylan Thomas' poetry, not only because he rolled the English language into a Rizla and set light to it, but also because he attended the same school as my father. The poem ' Do not go Gentle ' was written about Dylan's father; D. J Thomas, who was their English master at Swansea Grammar School. They shared the same view; the Thomas's from Cwmdonkin Drive and the Owen's from Dunraven Road, Sketty - both overlooking the 'green bay' of Swansea, that is often compared to the bay of Naples it stretches west towards Mumbles pier which snakes along the horizon into the sunset. Also, my mother used to babysit for Fred Janes, the painter who like Vernon Watkins, Wynford Vaughan-Thomas, etc., were forever grouped with Dylan Thomas as some kind of Swansea arty-bohemian movement at that time.)

In our shed to make a good working space, firstly, we had to create a window at the end to overlook the view, and also to let in the north light. This meant knocking a sizeable hole in the concrete block wall, but I was slightly worried that this might make the whole structure fall down.

We bought a concrete lintel from the builders yard and propped up the roof (just in case). Laurie and I then took it in turns to bash out a hole in the wall - just a long horizontal slit for the lintel, first of all. Once that had been cemented in place, we could safely remove a larger window shape under it.

With the first blow, the chisel pierced a peephole in the thick concrete block wall. Although outside, the view is all encompassing, there was something particularly tantalising about this tiny view. Putting an eye against it, suddenly it was easier to really focus on small details within the landscape; it was just like being inside an over-sized box Brownie camera. The hole allowed a tiny laser-beam of light to puncture the dusty darkness, as bright as Michelangelo's lightening streak on the Sistine Chapel ceiling.

We then took it in turns, smashing the ' landscape ' out of the wall and revealing that view inch by stunning inch - more exciting than painting - it was creative destruction. We were slowly turning a boring concrete space into an observation post; the land outside seemed to fall away from the new hole as though the shed was taking off. Being right on the edge of the land gave the small shed the feeling that it was gliding over the valleys below like the golden eagle. The humble potting shed had suddenly been elevated to Angel status.

Once the lintel had been set in place, a bigger hole was made under it and the edges smoothed. I made a wooden frame out of some wood salvaged from the *cantina* and we found (after another day's search), a place to buy a piece of glass on the outskirts of Fabriano.

Painted a bright white inside and with the addition of a worktop at the window end, it became our studio. A perfect space to paint, cool in summer with its thick concrete pan-tiled roof under the shade of the fig tree and really warm in winter with the addition of a little fan heater… and every time you looked through the new window, you were flying again.

Having somewhere to lay out our paints was as important as having a place to hang our hats. For us, it was the final piece to make this home a place where we could live on equal terms with Chalford. A studio, for a painter, is more significant than just a physical space; it is the place one goes to contemplate and soothe the mind. It is almost as important as the paint and canvas. It's somewhere to germinate the embryos of ideas. Achieving the right ambience in one's studio is as important as a well lit greenhouse, so that it can become the seedbed for 'bringing on' that elusive finished product. The initial ideas may not turn into paintings for many years, but can be placed for incubation in a studio.

It's not only the studio and the landscape that nurture the imagination, Le Marche is packed with inspiring works of art, even though it may not have the same recognition as some other parts of Italy. There is so much to admire that the artistic heritage is probably rather taken for granted by the locals. Enter a provincial art gallery or church, anywhere in Le Marche, Umbria or Tuscany and you're quite likely to find some little gem that for most other countries would be a prized treasure. Even our little town of Arcevia has an amazing Signorelli altar piece.

If just one tiny fragment of something from the Renaissance was found in a church in Barry, Banff or Broadwoodwidger, imagine the fuss that would ensue. It would certainly immediately be displayed in the National Gallery.

One of the most spectacular art treasures. I've ever seen is in the small gallery at Pergola, just up the road from us. It is called the *Bronzi Dorati*. Entering the room where it's displayed is a theatrical as well as an artistic thrill. As you open the door, the spot lights come on to light two life-size gilded bronze horses and figures. The exquisite Roman bronzes, which date back to the first century BC, are placed on a high dais in front of you - and they take your breath away. The shining, gilded bronze horses (although much of the gold has worn away) are every bit as exciting as the four bronze horses in St. Mark's, Venice - (the original ones are tucked away inside and were also once gilded of course), yet they are virtually unknown. The fine detail of the fig- ures has been observed with the precision of a diamond cutter. There's a satisfyingly realistic turn to the rider's legs as he grips the saddle and his fine boots actually appear to be 'worn' on the sculpted feet. It is illusion of the highest HD quality. And yet these figures were alive and well more than five centuries before the Renaissance. The detailing on the horses' bridles (like the tiny, helmeted warriors) and even the personality of the individual horses with their different facial expressions and angle of ears, the wrinkled hide around their necks ... and on the mane, from about a third of the way down the hairs change direction - all perfectly observed and sculpted with tremendous dexterity. It has been captured with a touch every bit as masterly as a Camilliani or Torrigiano. Yet this master is unknown. But the most extraordinary thing of all about this treasure is that the bronzes were ploughed up by a farmer in 1946; It makes one wonder what else might be out there, buried just beneath the surface?

Artists were certainly thickly-spread above ground in our area during the Renaissance; Gentile da Fabriano obviously came from Fabriano, the Salimbeni brothers lived in San Severino, Luca Signorelli painted several masterpieces in the vicinity, Carlo and Vittore Crivelli and Lorenzo Lotto also lived and worked in the Marche.Then there are the even bigger names listed in the defining work by Georgio Vasari; ' Lives of the Artists,' which catalogued a kind of premier league of artists in 1550.

Raphael's family lived in Cagli and then moved to Urbino, where he was born. There is a painting in a church in Cagli by Raphael' s father, Giovanni Santi, in which one of the angels is thought to be a portrait of the young Raphael. Also to Urbino came the two painters who, after Masaccio's influence, put a new perspective on perspective: Paolo Uccello and Piero della Francesca.

The most fantastic thing for us, as painters, is the availability of such treasures. It's possible to pop in to see an inspirational part of the Quattrocento on the way to the supermarket; it turns the mundane into the *magnifico*.

One of our favourite adventures is to follow the 'Piero Trail' all the way to Arezzo. Piero della Francesca's incredible paintings are dotted about en route, from Urbino to Monterchi and Sansepolcro then onwards to the newly restored fresco cycle in Arezzo. The trail of paintings include the ' Flagellation of Christ ' in Urbino, on to Sansepolcro to see the ' Madonna della Misericordia ' and the 'Resurrection of Christ' (regarded by Aldous Huxley as ' the greatest painting in the World ' – although as an innocent put down, a local child at primary school was heard to say, " so has he seen all the paintings in the world".) At Monterchi is the most unusual of all the paintings; the beautiful 'Madonna del Parto' (Madonna in Labour, or as we were told, the 'Pregnant Madonna').

The crowning glory of the trip is in Arezzo at the church of San Francesco; it is a whole frescoed end of the church depicting the Legend of the True Cross. When we first saw it fifteen years ago, it was possible to walk close to the original unrestored work high up on scaffolding. Although it has now been restored and can be viewed as a whole, I feel privileged to have been able to have seen the 'true painting' of the 'True Cross', so close I could see the brush work.

There was another interest, besides the Piero paintings on our expedition to Arezzo, as I mentioned earlier with our hoopoe experience; our children used to enjoy spotting the many colourfully dressed African prostitutes standing by the side of the road on the ' Piero Trail '.

Fiona was so naïve the first time we drove along that route, she wasn't aware what they were up to, and said: "Gosh, it must be a good bus service round here, have you seen all the ladies waiting for buses?"

Urbino itself has one of the finest collection of paintings in the whole of the country, housed in Duke Federico da Montefeltro's *Palazzo Ducale*. It contains paintings by Raphael, Piero della Francesca, Melozzo da Forlì, Paolo Uccello, Timoteo Viti,Titian and many others. Every time we visit, most of all I marvel at the number of bricks that must have been hand-moulded in order to create the structure of the town itself, with its gigantic walls, facades, arches and towers.

In the *Palazzo* there are huge rooms that rival anything in Florence, Rome or Venice in scale and grandeur. By contrast however, one of the most interesting rooms is a tiny *studiolo* entirely covered in pictures made of marquetry. The verneers of wood are used to create clever studies of perspective; books on shelves, cupboards with doors that appear to be opened, small animals and musical instruments that all trick the eye like a 'Trompe Louis'.

When we were last in the Palazzo looking at the *Flagellation* by Piero, we found ourselves standing in amongst a group of Italian school children. Their teacher was pontificating in front of the painting. Meanwhile, unknown to the teacher, the British art critic Matthew Collings was filming behind the crowd of kids, probably making a TV programme, no doubt hoping to educate the UK about the painter. It was amusing to watch because the teacher, annoyed by the filmy-banter in the background, he suddenly shouted out in English; " Will you PLEASE be quiet at the back… I'm trying to teach here !"

In the town, there is one of our very favourite fresco cycles, by the Salimbeni brothers, it has been restored now, which I think is a shame because ten years ago you could still see all the graffiti around the base of it, like 'Guiseppe wuz 'ere 1596,' but sadly, it was obliterated in the restoration process, so it's gone forever. It seems a shame to ' tidy up ' five hundred years of the living history in that painting; it has deprived future generations of that fascinating bond with real people from the past… long live the Banksy's!

Being a university city, there is always something going on in Urbino and plenty of glamorous young people. There are various book shops and stalls selling enormous truffles in the season - there are sixteen 'tartufi' species found in the area; the famed tartufo bianco (white truffle) is still one of the most expensive foods (weight-wise) in the world. Even the less expensive darker varieties are very potent in flavour and a little goes along way, so all-pervasive is its taste. A tiny grated piece is enough to flavour a whole dish of pasta, and once you've been 'grabbed' by its individuality it can be quite addictive.

We have a favourite restaurant in Urbino, where we while away hours, eating and drinking the many free delicacies they insist you sample as an extra bonus to the meal you order. Apart from the truffles there are other local dishes like *passatelli* (pasta with breadcrumbs and Parmesan cheese), *piccione ripeno* (stuffed Pigeon), or *coniglio in porchetta* (rabbit with fennel). Followed by a homemade cherry liquor. So it's not just art that can transform your day; Wherever you go in Italy, food is the fulcrum on which every day balances. They take it seriously here, and why not? It is a good place to start if you want to earth yourself, readjust your *chi* or just fill your boots.

There is no need to go to a restaurant either; one can grab a *piadina* (unleavened bread with cold meats) from a snack-bar or, on market day, one can get a tasty roll filled with hot suckling pig and wild fennel, from a *porchetta* van.

It doesn't matter if you're heading for a day on the beach, city, field or mountain; in every season you can be sure that there will be somewhere to get a good meal. Last autumn, we went up into the freezing and deserted Sibillini mountains with Jane and Howie (from Ascoli Piceno). We found what looked like a private house, from outside. We were taken downstairs, it was like being lured into a den of vice. Surprisingly however we entered a long barrel vaulted room, and it was packed with people limbering up for their Sunday lunch. Limber they needed to be... generations were seated in waiting, from small babies to great grand-parents pushing ninety - all patiently waiting for a banquet that needed a certain inner strength to cope with.

We counted twenty-two separate plates of food put in front of us - course after course of the set menu (and we had refused the pasta so we wouldn't get too full, like we had at Maria and Giovanni's!) There were some dishes such as tripe that I tried a bit of, but didn't go for, but the majority of them were fantastic, including wild boar and joints of beef, grilled on a spit in front of a huge fire. The house red was a fruity *Rosso Piceno Novello,* the local new season's wine. It all had the feel of a jousting banquet, and it was especially warming on such a cold day. Outside, the heavy sleet kept falling... and it seemed as if most of the villagers were wisely indoors with us.

As well as being very rural, one of the most pleasant things about the position of our house is its closeness to the Adriatic. It's possible to see the sea from San Giovanni and if we didn't have a hill in front of us, we would see it from the house too. A day at the seaside is not just about buckets and spades either. Food is as serious a draw as the sand and the (usually undramatic) surf. The seven miles of ' blue flag ' beach at Senigallia is also a seven mile stretch of seafood restaurants and cafes. The Italians seem to think it's odd not to want to be packed together like grilling sardines under acre upon acre of umbrellas - but it's not for us. They look on us as being rather anti-social, I'm sure; for we have found one of the small areas on that vast seafront where it's possible to set up our own encampment in relative isolation.

We've tried most of the restaurants along the front and have never been disappointed. The ones furthest away from the town seem to be slightly better, perhaps they put in just that ' little bit extra' to draw people to them. If a restaurant is full of locals rather than tourists we all know it's a good sign.

What could be nicer to accompany the heat, the turquoise sea and lots of glamorous bathers, than a simple dish of fine *spaghetti alle vongole* and chilled house *prosecco* or a local white *verdicchio* from Jesi?

Further down the coast, south is the Conero peninsula - a rocky outcrop sticking out of the otherwise straight Adriatic coast. With its more interesting topography, the coast there is broken up into smaller, curving bays. The sea is pure colour-therapy; a perfect gradation from the palest aquamarine to the deepest indigo, all bouncing off the bright white rocks.

The small beaches and coves feel like the Gower, the west coast of Scotland or the Greek Isles. However, despite the natural beauty, come lunchtime, food is put above all else. From tiny shacks and beach bars (one of them was recently voted the 'best beach bar in the world' by The Guardian!) and from *piadini* snacks to serious linen nap-kined places, every taste is catered for. Food really is the glue of life here, and by the coast it is almost exclusiv-ely seafood. We've had a couple of the local seafood specialities at an Italian friend's house – *baccalà* - (dried, salted cod that takes at least two days to prepare) and *brodetto* (a fish stew made from precisely thirteen species of fish, no more no less). Eating good food together contributes to the closeness of families and even seems to make friends more affectionate with one another. They set aside time to eat and drink together. Alcohol is very much just an accompaniment. There is an unhurried quality to eating that is akin to time set aside for worship or contemplation by other cultures, and food seems to be treated with the same reverence.

There really is nothing as relaxing as wandering slowly in the heat, through the shady streets and churches of one of our nearby towns; Sassoferrato, Gubbio, Fabriano or further away, Assisi - we tend to save Assisi as a special treat to show friends, a place to explore with them. We usually arrive around lunch time, so eating takes up the first hour or so. The town is built on a steep hill, so we park at the top and enjoy slowly wending our way down through the narrow streets. There are shops which sell handmade shoes or other leather goods, then there are delis, and the ubiquitous touristy shops near the honey coloured-stone piazza with it's fine Duomo di San Rufino. The Duomo has a Romanesque facade and a particularly beautiful early rose window and is enhanced by naive animal sculptures on the front elevation. Carrying on down more ancient alley-ways, there is the main piazza, *Piazza del Comune*, filled with bars and restaurants under pale canvas umbrellas you are enveloped by regal architectural styles which literally over-lap each other around the square.

Down more steep streets, to Via San Francesco, one is almost magnetically drawn, as a pilgrim to the climax of the day; the huge Basilica and tomb of St Francis. Although I am not committed to any particular religion, I can see that being a nun or a monk in this place would make you feel 'you had arrived' ; they really seem to be in their element, at the epicentre of what they believe in. Unfortunately it was also the epicentre of the 1997 earthquake which caused part of the roof of the Basilica to collapse killing four and damaging a fresco by Cimabue and Giotto.

Fortunately the building has now been restored - my only wish is that I could experience the thrill of seeing it all for the first time. The overwhelming power of the massive fresco paintings by Giotto, Cimabue, Cavallini, Lorenzetti and Simone Martini covering every surface of the mighty double-decker church. Stanley Spencer had jested with Henry Lamb that the only condition that he would make, if forced to go to the Front in the First World War, would be that he could take his Gowans & Grey art book ' Giotto, The Basilica of Assisi ' with him in his tunic pocket.

Every time we visit, I'm reminded of the time Fiona and I tracked down the first meeting place of Cimabue and Giotto. It was on a bridge over a meandering stream, set in the middle of a golden wheat field in the Tuscan hills. Leonardo da Vinci described Giotto's family background as being so rustic that he came from a place in the mountains where only "sheep and goats lived". Giotto, a shepherd boy, was apparently sitting on the bridge sketching with a stick in the dirt, when Cimabue came across him. He recognised Giotto's talent from this dirt drawing and invited him to be an apprentice in his studio. It is incredible to think that this artistic triumph in Assisi would not exist without that chance meeting.

One Church has been built on top of another and the decoration of the walls represents more human effort than is possible to put into words - Is there another place on Earth more significant for such primitive, painterly ambition ? Each time I go, I find something new, it's impossible to take it all in on a first visit so it's almost better to let the overall effect wash over you. If you were a potential candidate for conversion to Christianity, I think this place would toss you over the edge and baptise you at the same time.

In a state of quiet fulfillment after seeing all that beauty and its sheer scale, the walk back to the car park is done in a semi-trance like state. Having a *gelato* half way up the hill helps to take your mind off the steepness of the climb. It may also help to cool the sensory overload from all that painterly exuberance.

Around Arcevia, there were once something like forty castles or small fortified hill-top towns. Only ten or so remain today, although there are signs of a fortified past everywhere. Dotted on a drive to the coast, high-walled settle-ments stand proud of the plain like suckers on a squid, each tightly packed with houses within the castle walls for protection.

It's interesting how much security of property is still one of the first things people think about, even in the construction of a new house. Before anything else is done, boundaries are made secure with gates and fences. It's almost like there is a deep-seated memory of marauding Huns or Goths and they are taking no chances.

In the view from our newly-made terrace, a couple of hills and vales away, is the tiny village of Caudino. Its church tower glows pink in the evening light. I was amazed to find that this seemingly insignificant little hamlet had an important place in history, because it was where the last and greatest battle of the Guelphs and Ghibellines took place. (Between 1200 and 1300, the Guelphs supported the Pope and the Ghibellines backed Frederick II of the Holy Roman Empire - after years of war, the Guelph's eventually won, exerting French rather than German power over the peninsular of Italy). It's strange to look out over what was such an historically significant battlefield; a place of such violence, and to now see only peaceful rolling farmland - so quiet indeed, that even a passing cloud is a sensory disturbance.

Following the road from Caudino for a couple of miles, the

most perfect hill village rears up like a lion rampant. ' Heraldically challenged ' Palazzo looks as though it's been erected as a film set for an epic of Courtly Love and Knights of Yore. It still retains an authentic shabbiness that is disappearing fast in Italy as EC money pours into the restoration of these earthquake damaged back-waters.

The hill-town is built on an outcrop of rock and if you look through the ground floor windows, many of the rooms are completely filled with cliff-face. The lower elevation is simply a facade, it's only function being to hold up the floors above. Palazzo looks like a structure resulting from a game of ' chance ' played by termites, it's almost as though the buildings had been hurled against the rock and the fortunate ones that stuck were built upon, in a many layered mound. The buildings clutch onto each other any old how, as if the great stack was put together in an evening, after a very drunken supper. The odd angles of the walls throw uneven shadows across the towering structure. A bit like Matera, it is as camouflaged as a Q-ship (a revolutinary idea in visual deception by the British Royal Navy in WW1) at dusk.

Yet another steep climb to the top of the village, through alley ways that sometimes lead to a small allotment then link with another traversing path and some just come to a dead-end, it is real-life snakes and ladders '. When the summit is eventually reached, the cafe is very welcome; it's a good time for an ice-cream whilst looking down on the valley. The view is a criss-crossed kilt-plaid of olives and vines, blues and greens crossing in lines, and wherever they merge, a new colour is made. It rests the brain to look out over such neat farms, everything is ordered and calm.

Italians seem to take immense pride in being organised in their farming methods. They discipline their land in a series of well-ordered seasons, from tidy wood-piles to neat stacks of round bales, placed in lines at the end of every hay field before collection almost to just to demonstrate to everyone around that the farmers are in control. It seems that even for the old-timers there is a desire to place the stooks with mathematical symmetry and each one has a square of fabric on top like a hat. Tools, and machines new or old are laid neatly out in the stilt-legged barns, perhaps also as a display for their neighbours to admire as much as for practical reasons.

Sometimes bigger hay stacks, like witches hats, are created around a long stake, as though they are about to be burnt, but this method of hay storage is being rapidly replaced by the circular bales. Mechanised farming, although forcing some fields to be enlarged, does not seem to have changed the respect the farmers have for the countryside and their tidy maintenance of it.

There are, however, always exceptions to the ' tidy ' rule; a farm near us has adapted to the modern changes in a far more casual manner. Finding the opening in the barn wall too small for the new and bigger round bales, the farmer has simply taken a chisel and crudely hacked out a larger hole. It looks just as if a cartoon character has been rapidly ejected!

The ploughing after harvesting is done with massive tractors which usually have caterpillar tracks. They daringly plough even the steepest slopes. This first, deep turning of the earth creates huge, heavy clods of soil that shine in the sun like big chunks of chocolate.

In the Spring, the land is gone over once more to create a finer tilth for sowing. Often, they work floodlit, through the night, either because it's cooler, or perhaps it's because the machinery is cheaper to hire from the conzorzio or coopertive for night use, or just easier to borrow - whatever the reason - we don't know but we certainly admire their work ethic. The same happens at the other end of the season when they come to harvest the sweet-corn, wheat, barley or sunflowers. The sounds of combine-harvesters fill the nights in September. The harvester is off-loaded whilst on the move, into trucks that run alongside like refuelling in flight, or the mating of giant dragonflies.

In our area, cattle are rarely seen in the fields during the summer, because it's so hot. They are kept in great barns to avoid sun-stroke. Only the bell-laden Marchigiana (an old Italian breed of white beef cattle) can still be seen, grazing freely on the heights of our local mountain, Monte Catria, but as that's over1,700 metres high (by the way Ben Nevis is only 1,344 metres), they are always cooled by the mountain breeze, and the pale skin and coat protects against sun-stroke.

From the end of the garden, we watch the movements of a flock of sheep as they follow their shadows over dry fields and across our view, in search of pasture worth grazing. The shepherd's voice echoes between the valleys as a lop-eared straggler is brought into line by a large white *Maremmano* sheepdog. The constant watchfulness will become even more necessary, I suspect, if my wolf dream becomes reality...

It is a farmed landscape around us and guarding each area of farmland there is a fortified hill town. Each is placed strategically to overlook and defend the rolling farmland below, like an antediluvian 'big brother'. There are many walled towns such as Loritello, Piticcio, Barbara - some are tiny, whilst others, like Ostra Vetere, can be seen from miles away, its domes and towers resembling the city of Oz.

There are many *feste* or festivals throughout the year, whether for wine, truffles, wild boar or just the changing seasons - it seems that there is little need for an excuse for a party. Certainly the summer parties rotate loudly through our various windows in the summer months after dusk, as each small town or village takes its turn to play host, and employ a DJ through the night (it must be a good place for employment if you can etch and scratch at a bit of drum and bass).

Then there are the more personal celebrations. A trail from church to a wedding reception can mean miles of tied ribbons that last for years on trees, posts and signs (some ribbons probably stay in place long after the marriages have dissolved these days!). After the wedding reception and all that food, the bride and groom still head to foot in 'Armani', are presented with a six foot square block of plaster which they seem to have to hammer and chisel their way through, despite the dusted suit, to find some kind of tiny ' treasure trove'.

The birth of children is celebrated even more spectacularly, outsized storks (bulky plastic ten footers) bearing baby bundles in their beaks are hired from garden centres and placed outside the fertile couple's dwelling. On the front of the house a newborn's name is spelt out in ribbons (pink or blue) or in the garden the name grows on a bank facing the road for all to admire, made with flowering plants, shrubs or even trees like a municipal flower display in a British seaside town. More traditionally pagan; a thirty, forty or even fifty foot shaved tree-trunk is embedded in the garden for a year (or more) on top of which a bicycle is placed for a boy, or a doll for a girl, also we've noticed that girls sometimes have many stemmed tree covered with pink ribbons (but maybe that's more affectation than pagan).

In the evening, Arcevia is a bustling place. Everyone is out chatting at one of the two bars in Piazza Garibaldi. On the night of the Football World Cup final, the whole town was out to watch the game on a big television, in the *piazza*. Just studying the way Italians relate to each other is interesting, and sitting outside the bar, watching people, is one of our favourite pastimes. It's noticeable how many times they touch each other - not just with the initial hug and kiss, but throughout a conversation.

In a meeting on the street between a teenage boy and an elderly man in a wheelchair, we watched the boy as he kept gently stroking the head of an old, balding man, almost without noticing and certainly without being embarrassed that his friends might see this blatant show of affection. There's always much joviality between the groupings of old men, who have probably been in this *piazza* for most evenings of their lives yet have never run out of things to say. I'm sure there must be a lifetime of petty animosities and arguments between them, but they don't show. They seem to take it in turns to pat a shoulder or pinch a wrinkled cheek, in jest. A man in his eighties prods at a brand new moped that a youngster's showing off, and for a moment, the elderly man's eyes light up; he too is sixteen once more. The old man pretends to cock his leg over the bike to the exaggerated noisy protests of the boy.

Italy and France, neighbours and friendly rivals, were playing in the football final. The anticipation slowly built before the kick off. For the fans, an arc of folding chairs was placed in front of the large, flat-screened television. How organised, we thought, and how generous of the town to get this together as free entertainment. We sat in place early, in the sunshine.

However, there was, unfortunately, one unforeseen flaw in the set-up; they hadn't calculated that the kick-off happened an hour before the sun went down, so no picture was visible on the impressive screen! The event for the town had turned into a big ' Radio ' match. There was panic, this was an unprecedented emergency, with national pride at stake. The town elders went into a huddle by the bar, deep in gesticulating conversation.

Then, one of them came up with a bright idea; they wrenched the little portable TV from behind the bar and brought it into the shaded side of the piazza. The event was a good way of bringing the town closer; hundreds of people had to get very close indeed in order to squint at the tiny screen. Being densely packed together is something Italians seem to really enjoy. It just improved the atmosphere.

Discomfort was completely forgotten in the end ...

because Italy won!

Oh the joy! The leaping, the hugging, the party poppering, the hooting of horns went on until dawn, even out in the sticks' where we live.

We've found the locals, not being used to seeing strangers, are not over-effusive when they first see you. In fact, they have an unnerving habit of staring at you without a glimmer of a smile. One could regard this as a good thing; maybe they don't wear their hearts on their sleeves or dish out effusive but insincere affection. Anyway, once they do know you, they seem pleased enough to see you - with this attitude at least you know what your receiving is genuine.

If you're fortunate enough to edge acquaintance into friendship, then they will do anything to help you out in a 'good neighbourly' way, like when Ido cleared a path through the snow to our house, or waters our plants when we're back in England, without us even having to ask him. Also, he never makes a big deal out of these kind gestures, and even seems embarrassed when thanked.

Now, sig.Tortaloni's face lights up when we meet him. Since the work on the house is over, our relationship is more relaxed and when we see him it's usually to collect our post (which he takes in for us, out of kindness when we're not there), pay our IMU (council tax), or to give him some of his favourite brand of cigarettes as a thank you.

Our most recent job with him turned out to be more complicated than expected; we had noticed a rather pungent drainy smell at the side of the house, whenever the loos were flushed. We tried to ignore it but it didn't go away and the ' summer of flies ' made us aware that we had to do something about it. When I tried to trace the source of the smell, my nose guided me across the track. Horror of horrors, the end of the pipe was visible in the undergrowth, dribbling what appeared to be raw sewage onto our neighbour's land. Not nice. I did a drawing of where the pipe was coming out, and we went to sig.Tortaloni's office.

His office is old fashioned in decor, brown and orange being his favourite colours; it feels like being inside a chocolate orange. There are no signs of the modern day, (apart from the wall-calendar with that day's date on it). All the filing is done by hand. Behind the office desk, the wall is covered with drawers containing his ' database' ; rows of bulging cardboard files. It is very reassuring when he goes into his cabinet and there are your records on real paper in a real folder. It's a feeling of solidity instead of just existing on a screen in a computerised memory-bank.

There is an enormous hand-operated calculating machine with big numbers on chunky buttons. It clicks and chings loudly as the partially visible levers and wheels connect with each other inside the Bakelite casing. In one corner there is an angled drawing desk, under an Anglepoise lamp, just like my father used to have, with pulleys to manoeuvre the large ruler over the plans. Next to it, a table is buried under layers of architectural drawings. The only thing digital in the whole set up is the digit used to flick the fag-ash.

The aroma takes me right back to school and the old art-room, a kind of musky blend of toil and tobacco that exerts a Pavlovian response from me that I must draw!

My art-work on this occasion, however, was the route of the sewage pipe. It seemed pretty unimpressive to sig.Tortaloni; he just looked up at us and said :

" So... what's wrong with that?"

"Well," I said, "it's not very nice to have the pipe draining onto Enyo's field, even if he doesn't know it's there. Also it's far too close to our house, I mean what about the smells and the flies, we've had enough of flies..."

"OK, leave it to me," sig.Tortaloni said: "I'll talk to Enyo."

We returned to England, hoping that the problem would be sorted.

On our next visit I was pleased to see that the pipe had been extended by about fifty metres, but it was still inside Enyo's field. Enyo had obviously approved of the arrangement. Strange, I thought, I don't think I would want someone else's sewage pipe draining onto my land.

We went to pay sig.Tortaloni for the work.

He asked us to sit down... he doesn't usually.

"There's some good news and bad news," he said, "the good news is that you do have a septic tank, we found it. So we had it emptied and it's working fine. Look, I took photos."

He handed us photos of our septic tank (it reminded me of the time we had our drains rodded at the chapel and the firm handed us a video of our drains. It was a movie that rivalled one of our holiday videos for the ultimate 'boredom flick'). sig. Tortaloni was delaying the bad news for as long as possible.

"And the bad news?" I asked

"Well it's nothing really - it's just... Enyo doesn't like having the pipe on his land."

"Oh no - I thought you were going to have a word with him before you extended the pipe?" I was annoyed. We had lengthened the pipe at considerable effort and expense. Now we had to do what should have been done in the first place.

"It's OK," Tortaloni looked contrite, as he groped in his shirt pocket for nicotine comfort, "I'll correct it... we'll just move the pipe onto your land -

I'll hire a digger!"

The garden had only just recovered from the last digger. I had bought a shiny new lawn-mower - they say pride comes before a fall. I remember standing on my green sward, looking at the stripes on the newly cut lawn and thinking " yep, this is the best looking lawn I've ever had ". The stripes on the flat lawn ran perfectly towards the edge of the garden, the little seating area and the view. The glossy green parallel lines just lead one's eyes into that vista, it was like an advert for grass seed...

We left sig.Tortaloni in charge of the job, it was better not to be a witness this time. He had promised to minimise damage by only using a mini-digger.

Actually, the whole thing could have been a great deal worse. They did quite a tidy job: they replaced a gate and fence neatly and the forty metre long trench they had to dig for the pipe through the garden had been filled back in. But there was now an earth scar across my once perfect lawn. In my eyes the lawn will never look as good again - the land has sunk where they dug the trench and although I've filled it with earth and grass seed, time and again, the dug line always shows as a bit of a gulley of a different shade of green.

I've learnt tolerance however, and maybe that is where this whole journey through a mid-life challenge has been leading... the fact is that just being here is a privilege - being here on the Adriatic coast, a place by the Med. he reality of it outweighs all minor problems. I suppose it's a state of mind reached by those old sages who achieve mental calm up a mountain somewhere. Anyway, I'm sure it's better for one's health to not let minor faults like an imperfect lawn get to you.

It's a been one step forward... and five steps back, all the way through the making of the garden; the initial top-soil disaster certainly didn't help - we had to live with the shiny clay garden for two years, but gradually 'Nature' has healed all. The grass has grown and now there is a lawn sweeping generously around the house. Where it's been too clayish and physically hard to turn the soil, to create herbaceous borders, we have allowed the garden to revert to grass, not out of laziness or lack of will, but we've just realised it's pointless fighting against the way the land and the climate wants to be. We've worked with nature to keep life easy and the result is a less manicured, more natural feel.

Fiona said it would take at least five years to make a garden and she was right. It has been that long now since we bought the house and a garden has grown almost without us noticing. It gets easier as we learn what we are up against each season. It also has to be a space that can be maintained by us being here for maybe a third of the year (broken up up into vistits). It really has become, out of necessity, a low maintenance garden and is slowly and organically ever evolving. The grass is a great backdrop through which starring plants are placed and mowed around. I've worked out that the grass only needs to be mown about four or five times a year. Twice in the spring, when it grows thickly, then once or twice in the summer, when it's hot and hardly grows at all and once when we put the garden to bed in late autumn. So that's five days work a year to keep the garden in a fundamentally kempt state - not too much work really.

We've planted eight cypress trees in the lawn, along with the olive it's the other tree that represents Italy to us and we know that they grow well in our type of soil because not far away, there is a whole hillside of them where they have self-seeded. It looks like the old Biblical illustrations of the Garden of Gethsemane.

We are half way up a mountain and most our plants are flourishing especially the 'old sages', but locals were doubtful that our precious solo olive tree would survive. We've wrapped it up in metres of insulating fabric each winter to help it settle in and, so far, it seems to be okay. It was planted to commemorate my father and so appropriately it has had to " rage, rage against the dying of the light" through the wild, dark winters. Every spring, Fi picks off the shoots at the end of each branch to help it thicken out, but we won't be going into olive-oil production any time soon... but it has come to represent the passing of life itself in our eyes and, as I've said before, it is the embodiment of all our dreams of creating a garden in Italy.

The garden has been designed so that we don't have the burden of too much weeding. The soil is also so heavily clayish that weeding is far from being a pleasure. The climate makes our soil vary from slurry to concrete in summer and winter, depending on whether it's drenched, baked or frozen. So, there are just two small borders cut out of the grass next to the kitchen. Here, Fiona has planted a range of herbs and salad leaves: rosemary, lavender, origano, mint, rocket, tarragon, thyme, basil and of course sage - all a few steps from the cooking pot.

There are also artichokes and a tiny pomegranate tree, sheltering under the large leaves of the fig tree, next to the studio. As for flowering plants, Fiona has been patiently using the seed gathered from one indigenous hollyhock that we inherited with the house. Because the original plant liked it here, its seedlings are thriving all around the house. There's something very satisfying about propagating what you already know can survive well in a certain environment. Capitalising on it, rather than just going out and buying lots of new plants. Of course, it's a process that takes many years, but with patience, it's possible to create a garden that looks as if it's in the right place... and meant to be.

Fiona takes cuttings of mallow or buddleia especially for the butterflies: from swallow-tail to marbled white; in fact she takes cuttings from anything that seems to be doing well in our situation, and within three years a whole bank is covered in them. We've planted scented waxy jasmine over a doorway, on a trellis and under a window, so that the fragrance fills the house, and also the more exotic oleanders and claret trumpet vines that scramble up the front pergola, which faces south and so hopefully will survive the winters. (added this bit after the winter... it didn't survive!).

We have even, ourselves, ' succumbed to plumbago.'

So far, the garden extends around the house (about an acre) and I've slowly turned the dense undergrowth at the top of the land into lawn, simply by chopping down the saplings, then strimming and mowing. Continual mowing will turn any piece of waste land into a passable lawn eventually. Grass is tougher than most weeds, so can survive being an inch or two high, whereas most weeds eventually give up. At the top of the land there is a small area of woodland. I strimmed a pathway through it and discovered an old grape vine growing, so I knocked up a bench with wood lying around and a very rudimentary pergola to support the vine and it's created an area to read quietly in dappled shade. It always stays cool because of the breeze through the trees.

One day, we might create a rambling pathway through the rest of the woodland, which extends from the house down a valley. Another six acres to play with, but managing it is a long way off and it may have to involve serious muscle from the younger family members. But there's no pressure and certainly no hurry. We have only just scratched our tiny mark into the landscape. But this is the biggest lesson we have learnt from of our journey… we have found that in middle-age it's good to let go of ambition a bit. Where once a few years ago we might have striven harder to make a more impressive, even formal garden maybe for others to admire, now we are content with a less manicured and natural look and can see even more beauty in it.

However, the other day, standing in same place I had stood five years ago on the cold March afternoon when we first saw the house, I again glanced back at the house (now in its rapidly fading pink glory), the lawn has once again become stripy after its many traumas, and I thought; at last, this house has turned a corner, aesthetically, and whilst not being exactly beautiful, it is at least no longer " dog-ugly ". And even if it does sometimes rain in August and it isn't a place for winter sun, I think this has been a full-on positive experience. The challenges and thrills it has thrown at us have certainly occupied our minds whilst our young left home.

As for the influence on our painting, Italy has always been a major building block in the foundations of both of our work. It also could be considered as the birthplace of painting itself. From an early age, one is aware of the painters of the Renaissance; the artists from that era set a benchmark that is impossible to compete with, but it is something at least to aspire to. Not literally, but in a more esoteric way, that striving for perfection - a strange, unidentifiable energy that enabled them to create works which seem beyond human capabilities, is ' in the air' here. Just being in the area where people like Raphael lived and worked is a physical, spiritual and artistic inspiration and we both derive a thrill from the same landscape that was his muse. To drink from the same source of light, air, landscape and *vino* gives us both an indescribable tingle.

We feel we are in the right place for us; it has been a kind of homecoming.

Fiona's work has always been informed by the intricate illuminations produced by medieval monks. She studied manuscripts at art college, but where the monks' subject matter was invariably religious, her inspiration is drawn from a passionate love of nature. For over thirty years she has refined her paintings, concentrating on the observation and detail of her natural history subjects. Her visionary landscapes are often surrounded by borders of flora and fauna, all set on a ground of pure Italian gold-leaf. The paintings take many months of intense work, building up layers of oil paint, then etching back into them, exposing the colours beneath. Her subject matter is always drawn from the natural world and each painting is a homage to it. Much like the making of the garden in Italy, it's a process of patient evolution. She gilds blocks of pattern, just like in the manuscripts that Dante would have seen when staying a few miles away, at Fonte Avellana Abbey. Her paintings exude a quiet luminosity and the gilded areas gleam like early frescoes or icons.

I have to thank my Aunt Rene for my lifetime in paint. Not only did she tell me about the stripy Venetian poles, she also gave me three old books on painters. The trilogy was called something like ' The Works of the Great Masters '. Colour illustrations were rare then, but it was a book with full-colour prints that filled every other page. They were made all the more tantalising by the inclusion of a piece of tissue-paper over every picture. Uncovering each page was like opening a box of chocolates. It was packed full of Great paintings which from the age of six I took to bed nightly for years and studied inch by inch. I learnt perspective without really knowing what it was, and noticed how different colours were used to convey a cool shadow or warm light, the secret code of painting. It was the kind of information that might have been picked up as an apprentice at an artist's studio in the sixteenth century in Urbino. I got to know the paintings as intimately, as a child these days might get to know their Ipod, Facebook or Wii.

All I try to do with my paintings is imbue them with as much light and atmosphere as possible. Trying to describe exactly, in paint, the colour of air in shade (an indescribable apricot grey), or air in light (also an indescribable apricot grey), is a continual challenge. I marvel that within the confines of a frame, a small world can be made; for me, it's a kind of visual alchemy to create a reality and atmosphere in two dimensions, just from coloured gunk in a tube.

Artists throughout history have tapped into this world of manmade light that comes from mere pigment : Vermeer (maybe because he conveyed so accurately what was 'back projected' onto his canvas, that it seemed full of air), Turner (because of the light in his echoed shadows - it's that apricot grey again) , Monet (he was better at conveying light in paint than anyone else... he knew it all), Clausen (by learning from Monet), Whistler (for his spacious, airy night scenes), Frank Stella (the border of colour created a visual infinity within the canvas) and Howard Hodgkin (making space by an optical illusion of dots and dashes). There are, of course, so many more, but these are the ones that spring to mind and cover several centuries... artists may be interested in many things, but for these particular painters, conveying space and air within their painting has interested them as much or more than the subject matter. To quote Pablo Picasso; " There are painters who transform the sun into a yellow spot, but there are others who, thanks to their art and intelligence, transform a yellow spot into the sun."

David Niven always had our best interests at heart, and was adamant that we should not give our paintings away too freely.To explain why, he related a tale to us that Picasso had told him; an art collector had been desperate to own something, anything, created by the great man. Eventually the artist relented, and the collector was thrilled - to actually own a ' Picasso ' at last was a dream come true. Meanwhile, Picasso was well aware that the collector's inter-est was more financial than artistic. So he took him to a beach and promised that the work of art would be exclusively for him to own (although he didn't specify for how long). Picasso drew a master-piece in the sand with a stick, signing it with his show-man's flourish.Then, agonisingly, the collector had to watch as the incoming tide greedily acquired the creation from him, washing it away.

Now that our exhibitions are as home grown as our vegetables, and we rarely show our paintings in London or elsewhere any more; we could possibly be considered parochial, but I feel that what we both do in paint has a quieter value - I think, (as Robin Tanner, the fine etcher of pastoral England did), that there will always be a place and a need for artists like us to capture the Earth's natural beauty with honesty and integrity…

and if we don't record it in paint for our generation, who will?

Some time after we acquired the house in Italy, I came across an old folio of Laurie's pastel drawings. He had done them from his imagination when he was about thirteen, long before we had discovered our particular bit of Le Marche. I looked at them with amazement and called to Fi to come and see.

"Look at these, I'd forgotten about these pictures…"

"But that's peculiar," Fiona said, " this is the hill opposite us, Monte Sant'Angelo in moonlight."

She sifted through the bits of paper; each one was like the landscape of our local Marche. " Wow, look at this - it's exactly like the view from the end of the garden, those swirling patterns in the wheat fields. And this… look at those tall, thin farm-houses. They're just like the ones opposite us. " It was as though each picture contained a little section of the view from the end of the garden.

Uncanny.

Laurie had, from somewhere in his imagination, created images that exactly represented our view. These were scenes of our particular part of Italy - not the archetypal Italian imagery like from La Foce - and all done years before we'd even dreamt of finding a place there…. It was very strange.

The pictures are now on the walls of the house in Italy, where they belong. Visitors always assume they were drawn from the windows.

It's always hard to find a climax for a story like this, which like life itself is on-going and ever-changing. It could be possible to invent an ending or pretend some catastrophe like an earthquake (always a strong possibility here!) another plague, or some sort of cataclysmic awakening in creative or religious terms - but that hasn't happened, and thankfully life goes on.

However, what recently happened to the olive tree is drama enough I feel; the olive, as I have already said, is a totem of Italy for us, and could be considered the focal point of the developing garden, growing alone against adversity at this altitude, facing the north wind. It represents more to us than just another exotic plant from ' the sunny lands ' - it stands for fruitful maturity or maybe even for a mid-term fulfillment; a flourishing phase of life... middle-age. It had fought hard to cling on to life through all the harsh winters, and had been nurtured by Fiona who was conscious of its quiet meaning to me (because of my father) – however, despite it having been cosseted in layers of fleece, the unthinkable tragically happened; in March it was cleaved in two by heavy snow and killed the very week my mother died. You can imagine the emotional and psychological turmoil engendered by this simple twist of Nature. I hacked off its withered remains and flung them into our view with a feeling of despair.

Surely this is no kind of ending to this tale of our Italian adventure, I thought (although maybe it is an end that would echo this era of generally negative attitudes); perhaps this story should just finish on a contemporary and fashionably cynical note...

But no.

Now it is May. Yesterday - just yesterday, I noticed new and powerful shoots springing out of our olive tree's tortured stump... and, they were reaching to Heaven.

I keep thinking of a conversation with Hjordis, sitting by the pool in her amazing garden on Cap Ferrat and reminding her how lucky she was to have Lo Scoglietto for the summers, the chalet in Switzerland for the winters and a pad in London just for fun.

She shook her head and, in a serious Swedish tone advised us:

"Darlinks, never buy a place abroad... it's such a fuckin' bore."

But that's the one thing it's not.

Acknowledgements:

With thanks to travel writer Peter Greene (author of " Le Marche – An insider's Guide") for his editorial help and guidance.

Also to Fiona Owen for her patience and constant enthusiasm, both during our little adventure and the writing of it!